Surveyor
Situation

The Life and Times of a native Yooper from Michigan's Upper Peninsula

JOHN MATONICH

FOREWARD

The following is a collection of stories I have written over the years about life and family. I hope these stories remind you of similar experiences in your own life. They are intended to make you remember special times and to make you smile. My hope is that you enjoy reading them as much as I have enjoyed writing them.

John Matonich

CONTENTS

ACKNOWLEDGMENTS

Special thanks to my wife, Stephanie for all her support and encouragement to make this book a reality and to Stacy for all her hard work helping me put the book together. I appreciate all the hard work and couldn't have done it without either one.

"Infomercials"

Sometimes I think that television has gone too far. It's not the "near-adult" programming that seems to be everywhere (although that is getting out of hand). It's not the political advertising that still has my ears ringing from the last Presidential joy ride. It is those 30 minute "programs from hell" known as the "infomercial". Surely, you know what those are. They sell everything from Nordic Trac to food dehydrators. Lately, though, I believe they have crossed the line.

I came in from my wood shop one Saturday afternoon to refill my coffee cup and found my children signing along with an infomercial promoting a Karaoke machine. I asked my 9 year old daughter how many more off-key renditions of "New York, New York" she could stand before flipping back to "Barbie World"? She just looked at me and said, "Karaoke is cool, Dad" and then gave me the "but you're not" look and started to sing along with the overweight balking television figure as he burst into "Bad Bad Leroy Brown". I gave up and went back to the sanctuary of my shop where the sweet music of machinery would certainly overwhelm any unwelcome noise from Elvis wannabees.

Later that evening as I was channel surfing, I thought I saw something that stopped me in mid-surf. It appeared someone was spray painting their head! I couldn't help myself, I had to wait and see what could possibly drive someone to do this. I soon found out it was an infomercial for a product for people that were "follically challenged" (going bald). It was being touted as a response to thinning or balding hairlines. The program focused on a dozen or so gentlemen each of whom submitted their scalp to a coat or two of this miracle spray. Every one of them said they felt younger and their significant other agreed as they stared at the results of the paint job. I was really waiting to see if any of these admirers would try to run their fingers through the remaining locks. It was obvious that they were not going to without a towel handy or at least until the lights of the studio baked it dry.

Peoples' continued drive to appear younger will never cease, but I hope someday we can look at the Emperor and tell him he has no clothes on (or at least no hair). Perhaps we can legislate that Infomercial hosts must try out all products to the point where we would see the day when someone would be singing "New York, New York" while using a Nordic Trac and spraying a balding head with hair paint...at least we could condense our viewing time.

And that's the situation as I survey it...

"Waiting is Frustrating"

Life is full of frustrations. This revelation came to me the other day as I stood in an express lane at a local store trying to buy a couple of hinges for a piece of furniture I was making. I wouldn't have come up with the profound vision except I had been standing in the same spot for 15 minutes. The reason I hadn't moved is because the person in front of me had a cartful of items and was trying to find a checkbook somewhere on their person. I looked above the register at the sign that read "Express Lane – 10 items or less-Cash Only", and could only shake my head as I watched the clerk ring up the Eleventy millionth item (yes, that IS a real number....especially in this situation,) and then have to call for a manager to approve the out of town check. After reading "War and Peace" (*which was being passed around to those of us standing in line,*) I was finally able to conclude my sale and exit the store.

On the way home I found out all about anti-lock brakes as a large black Buick pulled in front of me. I think I saw the name SS Tub of Lard painted on the side as it wheeled into the lane I was occupying. To make matters worse, the captain of this boat decided to turn right at the next block, and off he sailed into the abyss of some quiet neighborhood. After scraping my face off the windshield, I looked around and saw that there were no other cars in sight. I couldn't help but wonder why the captain of this vessel couldn't wait another five seconds for me to pass uninterrupted before he decided to enter the shipping lanes.

These are just a couple of examples of how you can get a bad hand dealt to you every now and again. Generally, there isn't much you can do and usually some type of response only makes matters worse. Believe me I thought about pushing Mr. "Those express lane signs don't apply to me" right out the door with my cart and poking holes in all his paint cans. I also gave serious thought to following the captain of the "cut in front of traffic" boat to his destination, making him surrender his license, and then torching it in front of him thus assuring the human race that his sailing days were over.

While these actions might lead to a brief feeling of satisfaction (well...maybe more than brief...) [*grin!*] they are really not things reasonable people do, so I have to satisfy myself with the vision only.

I had plenty of time to calm down on the rest of the trip home, and did manage to calm the side of the brain that is rooted in getting satisfaction by convincing it that the customer's check bounced and the store was in the process of chasing him down with those rent-a-cop parking lot security people they hire. I also had a vision of the Buick pulling out in front of an unmarked police car on his next voyage, and the policeman didn't have a sense of humor-and did in fact torch his license. They can do those kinds of things, so I'm told. Sometimes life can be good....

And that's the situation as I survey it...

"Garage Sales"

One man's trash is another man's treasure. I'm sure we've all heard that, but it is never so true until you or someone in your family decides to have a garage sale. This ritual of summer recently visited the Matonich household. My bride decided while there was still snow on the ground (which seems like last week) that this was the year for an "excess inventory sale". Not being one to rock the boat (at least not at home), I grinned and mumbled words of encouragement.

Somewhere about a month before the appointed time the intensity level started to increase. I found out this was not only going to include our expendable items, but those of two other families. I soon had to start answering questions about the validity of hanging on to things like old sweatshirts, old schoolbooks, and new motorcycles. "Now just a cotton-pickin minute, let's not get carried away", I said to my new retail wizard. The walls of our garage began to transform into display areas for home interior items and candle sconces (whatever those are). I walked into my workshop which is attached to the garage and found everything that wasn't going to be sold stored in there. After tripping over my kid's bikes for the 12th time while trying to work on a new project, I decided that I would wait until this bargain extravaganza was over and I could reclaim the sanctity of my shop.

During the course of setup, I would call home periodically to try to offer encouragement. I would get reports that Ellen and one of her friends would have just settled a discussion over whether to price an item 25 cents or 50 cents. Just being glad it wasn't me in the middle of that made my week. As the big day approached, the intensity level was at a fever pitch.

Adding machines and clipboards were in place. Items that survived the cut were either in my shop or covered sufficiently to avoid confusing shoppers.

At last, it was here…opening day. I left the house a little earlier that morning (4:30 am) to make sure I was nowhere to be found as daylight approached. I cautiously dialed my home phone number about 10:00 am and could only barely make out the *"whaddaya want?"* over the roar of the crowd. Evidently, people were lined up before 8:00 am waiting for the garage door to open. I said, *"Wrong number"* and hung up. Yea, I know I'm a chicken…but I wasn't about to become the vent pipe for any frustrations.

I quickly hurried home at the end of the day (I was able to squeeze an extra 30 minutes by FINDING a traffic jam), to discover that people were still there shopping. I thought it was to be over at 4:00 and by now it was 6:30 and stragglers were still haggling over whether the Barbie lunch box was worth 75 cents. I watched from behind a tree until I could spot my significant other. She seemed to be smiling, so I figured it was safe to approach. She told me that it was a great day, and although it was busy, she was happy at their success. So happy in fact that she stayed up until 2:00 am the following morning looking for additional items to replenish her depleted stock for the next day of the sale. She also began talking about the sale she is planning for the fall…I told her I thought November 15 is a good target day to shoot for [grin].

And that's the situation as I survey it…

"Sleeping Children"

It is about 8:00 pm. The room is dark. All you can hear is your own breath and that of the little figure below you. Only 30 minutes earlier that little figure was full of "p & v" (____ & vinegar...you can fill in the blanks), but now has drifted off to some faraway place where teddy bears are in charge and animal cookies pave the streets. You turn to walk away and it happens...that squeak in the floor you have been meaning to fix somehow finds its way beneath your foot. The noise made would deafen a brass band (at least it sounds that way in the quiet dark) and then you hear the two words that make your blood run cold... "Da Da". You turn around and see that smiling face that makes all the troubles of the world dissolve into meaningless drivel. You shrug your shoulders, turn back to the crib and start patting her back once again.

My daughter is well beyond this stage, but a number of us were discussing the latest methods of child rearing during lunch the other day, (we are lucky to have several new parents) and the memories of trying to get my daughter to sleep came flooding back. I may not have smiled much then, but I sure do now remembering it.

My son was never a problem to get to sleep. You tell him it is time for bed, and Matt pretty much marches up the stairs without a whine. His sister, Katelynn, on the other hand would never go to sleep if she wasn't ordered to. She is forever trying to make a deal for an extra half hour today in exchange for going to bed a half hour earlier tomorrow. It's amazing how many times she forgets about that deal the next day, and equally amazing how many times her mother doesn't.

It has been and continues to be a joy to watch those two curtain-climbing, ankle biting, little rug rats evolve into contributing members of society. We all agreed as we discussed our offspring that although problems exist at all ages (just ask my mother), we wouldn't want to go back. The joys of watching them grow, and the pains too, make it worthwhile.

But I may have to re-think that. My secretary just came in to ask if she could leave for a few minutes because her 19 year old son called her collect from Kentucky and asked her to wire money so he can see another concert and have enough gas to get home. Maybe "Da Da" forever isn't so bad......

And that's the situation as I survey it...

"Take a Drive"

"See the USA in your Chevrolet..." is a portion of a jingle that is as much a part of Americana as 4th of July fireworks. If the music to this advertisement isn't currently running through your head you have to be younger than 35 or have never watched Sunday night television in the 60's. I can remember huddling around the TV hoping that Walt Disney showed a cartoon and not some stupid show about a coyote living in downtown Los Angeles. Even the Love Bug held more entertainment value to me than salmon swimming upstream in some remote river while a grizzly tried to catch supper.

Of course, after Disney was the most honest, upstanding, hardworking family on TV....no, not Roseanne or the Huxtables, but the Cartwrights. Ben, Little Joe, Hoss and Hop Sing. There was an older brother but he left to make his fortune early in the program's life with only an occasional cameo appearance (probably corresponding to his BMW payment.) It was during this program that the Chevrolet Motor division of General Motors convinced America to vacation all over the country by piling in the family wagon or sedan and heading somewhere.

This marketing plan was very successful. Car sales rocketed and families did spend their time together squeezed in between suitcases and sleeping bags. My wife, her mother, father and five brothers and sisters went out west not once, but twice. To this day she can't ride backwards in a vehicle because she and her sister rode in the far back seat of a station wagon facing to the rear all the way to Pike's Peak. While my family didn't travel too far from home, we did take "Sunday drives" regularly. This consisted of local trips through the countryside on Sunday afternoon with Mom & dad in the front and the kids in the back. During the fall, we would listen to the Packer football games on the radio and look for deer and partridge. Only in the UP can road hunting be a family event (*grin*).

All this traveling came to a screeching halt when OPEC decided that they needed a little more jingle in their pockets and the price of a gallon of gas went from $0.30 to $1.50. Big cars, long trips and the Cartwrights went by the wayside and the country was destined to drive vehicles that could barely hold two adults and a cup of coffee, let alone a growing family. Chevrolets were replaced by Hondas and Toyotas. Definitely a setback for countryside travel.

Today, gas is more reasonably priced and big cars are back. They get great mileage and can fit a growing family and their luggage as well. There is also a reemergence of the desire to explore America. More people are traveling the back roads as well as the expressways in search of Americana. I hope this doesn't ever change. Start by taking a different way home from work or school. Get off the main highway and take a rural road. On Sunday, go for a drive with your family or sweetheart (road hunting is optional). Visit the sites of interest close to home first before venturing outward. There is a lot to see and do and you will be surprised on how well you will communicate with the people traveling with you. Even your kids will at least ask "are we there yet?" It may be the most you have heard from them all week, but it's a start. Just don't make them ride backwards up to Pike's Peak…they will never let you forget it.

And that's the situation as I survey it…

"Customer Service and Special Gifts"

Is it just me or is there a big swing from bad to good on how we get treated by people from that most famous oxymoron called "customer service". You know what oxymorons are…phrases like military intelligence, or postal service (I can now say that without fear of being slugged since my significant other has "retired" from the Post Office..but that's another story)….Anyway, having just finished the largest retail adventure of the year known as Christmas we are all probably too familiar with the process of returning presents that just were not quite right. Things like those zodiac book markers with the built-in reading light. They work very well in a dark room, but are hell on the book bindings. Another gem is the 101 Dalmatians bedroom slippers you got from Aunt Sally who can't seem to remember that you're not a 5 year old anymore. The worst, though, could be the Wayne Fonte's autographed football…he thought he was signing a lunch box which may explain a few of his problems. As you can tell, all of these lead to a trip to the return line.

I have been lucky over the years in either getting things that I have wanted, or have been able to fake how much I liked the fluorescent yellow sweater in extra tall…then bury it in the far corner of the "never open" drawer. I may have to make a ceremonial appearance with it on but usually it is at a family gathering where everyone else is wearing something close in style and for the same reason. Only glances are exchanged with the understanding that this attire will have a merciful and quick ending.

On the few occasions that I have had to request a refund or exchange, the reaction has ranged from "we're sorry it didn't suit your needs, here is some money" to "what possessed you to want a football autographed by Wayne Fontes, anyway?" I never know what to expect until I venture to the land of the misfit items. The customer service representative's attitude is generally proportional to the length of the line. It also is affected by the attitude of the person directly in front of you in line. If the person in front of you goes into a litany of why his foot massager didn't quite fit their dainty feet (you thought they were snowshoes...) and the clerk starts to roll their eyes back in their head (a sure sign of trouble), you could be in for a rough time of it when it is your turn.

Whenever you have to return something or use customer service, please remember one thing: No matter how difficult it is, no matter how long you have waited in line or have been on hold, do your best to be upbeat. Remember the clerk you are facing has probably been there longer than you have and has already given returns on who knows how many Wayne Fontes autographed footballs.

And that's the situation as I survey it...

"Someone Upstairs"

As a boy growing up in the wilds of Michigan's Upper Peninsula, my parental education was probably not much different than anyone else. I vividly remember my mother's explanation no matter what went wrong. Her response to my predicament was usually, 'I told you not to do that" or "someone upstairs punished you for that". This also falls into the category of "You'll poke your eye out" or "shoot your eye out". So far I still have all my fingers and both my eyes so I guess all of this training has paid off. I must admit, though, there have been many times that I felt as though someone upstairs punished me.

I remember one instance in kindergarten where one of my classmates came to school wearing something out of the ordinary, (such as a non JC Penney pair of pants.) Some of my classmates and I took great pleasure in ridiculing the poor kid until he was near tears. Keep in mind that this doesn't take much at that age. I should have remembered my mother's sound counsel and not been a part of this harassment because, true to her prediction, when I sat down for music time just a few minutes later, I failed to realize that the fly on my JC Penney Levi wanna-bees was open. Even more unfortunate, this situation didn't escape most of my classmates. As you can imagine, guess who became the next target? Still puffy-eyed when I got home, I ran to my mother looking for solace. She comforted me with a big hug. This treatment still works today except I substitute my bride as the hugger (since Mom is 500 miles away & Ellen hugs pretty good too.) Mom also poured me a big glass of whole milk and gave me a couple of freshly baked chocolate chip cookies (today that would equate to 1% milk and fat free Snack Wells). Everything was going great until she found out I was part of the first group of harassers and all the motherly soothing went out the window. I then got the speech about someone upstairs punishing me for being mean.

I'm afraid as I grew up, I probably didn't learn very quickly, as I heard those speeches plenty. From playing with sulfur and matches when I knew the consequences, (I've got the scars to prove it) to copying Evil Kneivel by riding my pedal bike over an incline not meant to be jumped. That trip cost me three days in the hospital which really gave me a lot of time to think about mom's philosophy.

In adult life, I do try to remember how anyone's actions can affect others...good or bad. I try to remember how we treat others should always be tied to how we want to be treated. I continually try to remember that as I am faced with life's little challenges. I'm afraid, though sometimes I forget. Just the other day we were teasing one of our staff for his choice of sweaters. I didn't think much about it until I got home for dinner and both my wife and daughter burst out laughing. When I asked them what was so funny, they said my tie wasn't even close to matching my jacket. I tried to explain that happens when you get dressed in the dark so as not to wake the family, but they weren't buying it. I then thought about the ribbing we gave the guy at work over his sweater and I could hear my mother's voice all over again. At least my fly wasn't open...I know because I checked....

And that's the situation as I survey it...

"That Golf Thing"

At the risk of being clubbed with a "Big Bertha", I have to ask, "What is it with this golf thing?" It is now moving into the best weather of the season and all around me the conversation is centered on some little white ball and the effort it takes to knock it into a little hole in the ground. Don't get me wrong, I like sports as much as anyone, but I guess growing up in an area that never seemed to have much in the way of summer, (we used to refer to it as 6 weeks of bad skiing), golf was never much of an option. I spent my youth playing ball…you know, foot, basket and base…along with most of my peers, so I was not exposed to this game until later in life.

I have tried to play the game; I even took a few lessons, but have never found it to be anywhere near as relaxing as it is told to be. I always found that my clubs traveled farther than the ball. It is however, kind of cool riding around in a cart, but the course officials don't appreciate it if I just try to sightsee instead of playing the round. Besides, it is usually difficult to find someone to race with as most golfers are so blasted serious about what they're doing.

Probably the only thing more difficult for me than playing golf is trying to watch it on TV. The hush falls over the crowd as the player reaches in his bag for a wedgy iron or whatever and immediately you can read the minds of all the spectator pros that are second guessing the selection. If the shot goes astray you can see them all turn to each other in the gallery with the "I told you so" look. If it is a great shot, then obviously that's the club they would have chosen. It also gives me a headache when they continually flip back and forth between different holes and different players. Next thing you know, they will have a screen pen for the commentator to use in a reverse angle camera so you can have a better view of the ball plopping into the water.

I also have a hard time getting excited about the variety of equipment that has to be purchased to even play the game. It seems to be marketing in the purest form when they can convince the buying public that the $500 set of irons that you bought last year are certainly no match for the krypton shafted silk wound set that is being introduced this year. *But of course,* they will throw in a sleeve of balls and a hat with the latest trademark. In all fairness, this hat trick works on most men who buy anything (just ask my wife).

Maybe if they allowed cheerleaders or marching bands at the golf matches I could stay more interested. Or if they had low priced bleacher seats and sold bad hot dogs or stale beer. Perhaps if they had a rule that after a shot your opponent could run down the fairway and grab your ball and throw it back before you reached him and blocked him, it would be more fun to watch. I know it would be more fun to play! It could be a start to a whole new line of athletic gear, and I sure would have a better reason to throw my club down the fairway.

And that's the situation as I survey it...

"Big Baby"

In today's world of "macho" men I have to confess...I'm a baby! That's right. I've discovered that this 6', 240 lb. slayer of all that life has to throw has been reduced to a mere shell of a man. What could have caused this transformation? No, it wasn't a run-in at some faraway place with folk that don't appreciate my Harley. That would have been easy. In fact, I could tell you about the time...nope I better not...I'll just keep that one to myself. It wasn't my family either, although my knees still go a little weak when my wife walks by and winks. The reason for this change is the sound of the dentist's drill.

Before I go on, I would like you to think of the face you just made when you read the words "dentist's drill" and perhaps you know what I mean. I have had to have some dental work done recently and just the thought of it sent me into spasms...that is, until I got to the dentist's office. Once I got there, my whole attitude changed. Mind you, I was still a baby, but all the wonderful folks there understood and let me be a baby without so much as one "be a man" or "you can stand a little pain". In fact, they made the entire experience very pleasurable (I guess as much as anyone could, considering they had to probe, and prod and drill). The whole time I was at ease and felt comfortable. I believe this was helped by the two and a half tanks of laughing gas I sucked through my nose, and the multiple shots of Novocain that made my mouth feel like it did after the Harley incident I mentioned earlier.

I think the important lesson I learned here is that I wasn't afraid to say I was afraid and the good folks at my dentist's office worked with that. Admitting this is not easy for me (or for most males of the species.) It is just like men asking for directions. I have told my wife several times that I have never been lost...but she knows that I have been seriously bewildered a couple of times. As hard as it was, I'm glad I told them I was a baby.

I do think this feeling is only temporary, because as soon as the Novocain wore off, I was back to "Al Bundy" mode. Fearless, restless, and needing a shower from the sweat. I have found that the after effects are limited. I do get a little teary watching my kids grow up, but I still don't want to watch the "Bridges of Madison County", so I guess I'm safe for a while until the next visit to the dentist when I have to say, "Hi, I'm John, and I'm a baby..."

Post Script – I proofed this article again before submission after spending two days in the hospital because of some complications after oral surgery. My feelings are unchanged. All the folks involved were top-notch and let me be the baby I am.

And that's the situation as I survey it...

"Hometown Pride"

While I was back in my hometown for a visit during the fourth of July, I had a couple of experiences that reinforced my love for small towns. Don't get me wrong, big cities have a lot to offer, but it is small town America that always tugs at my heartstrings.

I was riding with one of my brothers in his truck (red, with a gun rack, of course...) when we pulled up to a stoplight. Yes, there is ONE stoplight in my home town. I don't think it is needed, but what the heck, it gives everyone a reason to stop at the intersection. While we were waiting our turn for the green light, another truck went through the intersection and the driver waved at my brother. As we drove down the highway, other drivers coming the opposite way waved as well. This made me remember while growing up how everyone in town would recognize each other's vehicle and wave. You don't see much of that in the more urban areas. Usually, if someone waves at you, you look to see if they are just using their hands while talking on a cell phone or if your car is on fire. The longer I was home, the bigger the smile I got when people waved. It didn't seem to take very long before I was right back in the same groove I was before moving away. I don't have a gun rack in my wife's Blazer, but it is red...(*grin*).

I also got a big case of hometown pride the day before the Fourth of July celebration. I was at a class reunion gathering where I ran into people I hadn't seen since graduation. We had 85 people walk down the aisle to get their high school diplomas, and as I got caught up on what had gone on since graduation I realized just how well my classmates had done. About every profession was represented as well as many people skilled in the trades, crafts, and just hard workers. Some had left the area, as I did, but you could tell the hometown roots were strong and deep. The caliber of the people that came out of our local school system was further reinforced when the newspaper announced the grand marshals for the next day's parade. They were both graduates of the same system my classmates and I were. One was a US Congressman from Wisconsin and the other was the Chief of Surgery for the Mayo Clinic in Rochester, Minnesota. You could tell how proud the town was of these two as they rode past during the parade.

I'm not sure how my hometown stacks up against any other, but I don't believe comparison is important. What is important is being proud of your roots and what you can do with your life to make not only the town you're from, but also where you live today, proud to call you its citizen. Maybe it should start with a wave to your neighbor or someone you see very day at the same stoplight. Hopefully, they will wave back and not look to see if their car is on fire.

And that's the situation as I survey it…

"The Big Game"

I recently had the opportunity to take my eight year old son to a professional football game and found it to be an interesting experience. It had been quite a while since I had been to a pro game, but it wasn't long before I remembered why. It happened to be one of the biggest games of the year: The Green Bay Packers versus the Detroit Lions. Now, I am neither a Packer nor a Lion fan, but one of my brothers and my brother-in-law contributed to the delinquency of a minor by corrupting my son into becoming a Packer fan. In fact, you could say he is "green and gold" through and through. This is much to the dismay of his father, who has been a Chicago Bear fan for most of his life.

You have to keep in mind that where I grew up, Vince Lombardi walked on water and life comes to a halt on Sunday afternoons while the Packers play. I was home for a visit this fall and the big news was that the Packers had a week off. It meant all the menfolk could stay at camp preparing for the upcoming fall deer hunt without fear of missing a single play. The locals were upset when Fox television got the contract for pro football because you can only get a Fox channel via cable TV. Even though most of the camps have a television of some sort, cable is about as prominent as indoor plumbing. This means Sunday afternoons during football season have to be spent in town rather than in the woods, which goes against a hundred years or so of male genetic evolution in the Upper Peninsula of Michigan.

My son, Matt, and I arrived a couple of hours early for the game just so we could walk around the parking lots at the Pontiac Silverdome and observe all the tailgating going on. It was obvious to us very quickly that tailgating has become a science. Most of the folks were well equipped to be as comfortable as possible while they were preparing for the game and the smell of barbecue grills was everywhere. It was also fun to look at all the clothing that detailed the allegiance of the wearer. We met a lot of people who had made the trip from Green Bay and of course, they befriended my son quickly as he approached with his Packer garb on. I let him display his "colors", but we kept it toned down a little, especially since we had gotten tickets on the 50 yard line behind the Lions' bench. I really didn't want to overly excite any of the die-hard Lion fans that usually roost in that same location.

The heartburn of any game in an arena such as the Silverdome is always the same. First, you have to mortgage your house to get the tickets. I was fortunate enough to know someone who couldn't use their season tickets for that game and didn't have to deal with the on-site ticket dealers…better known as scalpers. I saw some of those deals go down and it wasn't a pretty sight. Once inside, we were bombarded with vendor booths selling every piece of paraphernalia known to man with a Lions or Packer emblem. I escaped relatively unscathed by getting Matt a small Packer pin which he still proudly displays. Although we had a good breakfast that morning, we did get hungry and wandered over to the nearest food concession. After shelling out $25 for a couple of brats, some nachos, and a couple of pops, I had to ask if I was now a shareholder in the food stand rather than just a customer. The vendor, while trying to half smile, gave me the look that said, "Oh yeah…real funny…like I never heard that before." We retreated to our sets and watched the rest of the game. A lot of the day's entertainment came not only from the game, but also from the fans. Many cheeseheads, painted faces and banners were all around the stadium. And those folks were sober...so you can imagine what the heavy tailgaters were like.

Even though the Packers lost that day, (a game they should have won), Matt and I had a great time. His eyes pretty much stayed wide the entire game, especially when his favorites were on the field. I even caught him clapping for Barry Sanders. When I asked him about it, he said it was just so much fun to watch him run. I had to agree with him, but it was more fun to watch my son at his first pro football game. It may have cost a few bucks, but I forgot all of that when on the way back to the car he gave me a big hug and thanked me for a fun day. Maybe these brats weren't so expensive after all.

And that's the situation as I survey it...

"Air Travel"

I have a real love-hate relationship with traveling by air. I love to travel by plane, but hate the fact that the lords of the air usually find a way to make my trip as close to miserable as possible. I don't travel as often as many others, but I have sure had my share of bad luck (at least that's what the airlines call it).

I was flying back to Michigan a while ago from Madison, Wisconsin. I don't remember exactly why I was in Madison, but I'm sure it had to do with cheese or the Packers or Harleys or something like that. Anyway, I got to the airport in plenty of time to discover all the flights to Michigan that afternoon were canceled. The sun was shining and there were no picket signs in sight so I was at a loss to understand why I wasn't able to get home. The poor ticket agent wasn't making any friends either trying to explain it to the 25 or 30 people all trying to get back to Michigan. He was finally able to reroute me on another airline. My wife couldn't understand how I was going to get home when each time I called her it was from a location closer to California than to Michigan. Finally, after several plane changes and a fine tour of the Western US, I arrived back home. I chalked it up to a life experience and didn't let it stop me from flying again.

Maybe it should have. One of the next times I flew, I was on the very last leg of a long trip which meant getting out of the reasonable comfort of a jet and into a "turbo-prop" plane that was to fly from Detroit to Flint. I'm not sure, but I think "turbo-prop" is French for "over-stuffed sardine can with wings". As with most of the commuter flights from anywhere to anywhere it was full. I got one of the last seats in the back by the window. I sat down just in time to see them unload some luggage from the baggage compartment. Evidently, some of my fellow passengers had those extra peanuts they offered and we were now too heavy for those "turbo-props" to get us off the ground. Not liking the alternative, I saw the wisdom in this decision. Unfortunately, two of the bags left behind were mine. I waved them good-bye as we taxied down the runway. I had to wonder just what cities they would see before they finally made it back to my home.

I guess lost luggage and canceled flights are a small price to pay for the convenience of air travel, but sometimes I have to wonder. I've never lost my luggage in the truck of my car nor have I had my car leave without me. Even though it doesn't serve peanuts, there is no better way to travel than on the back of my Harley... now if I could only fit it with wings.

And that's the situation as I survey it...

"Advertising"

Sometimes it irks me when advertisers are stereotypical. I mean come on…is it always necessary to make assumptions when they select the appropriate medium for their ads? For example, I was having lunch the other day and the restaurant had ESPN playing on the TV. In fact, they were showing highlights of the Senior Golf tour. Now, if I have the choice to watch golf over grass growing, I most times would choose the grass, but the rest of the diners were content with the golf. When it came time for the commercial, it was announced the program was brought to you by Cadillac. I had to wonder if advertisers think if you can afford to watch the senior tour on your lunch hour, you must be able to afford to drive a Cadillac. That might be possible, but I didn't see any one of the patrons in the restaurant paying much attention to the ads. In fact, I swear I saw a couple of folks glance outside to check the length of the grass. I wonder if any more attention would have been paid if the ads dealt with plaid pants or funny hats or some other type of golf paraphernalia.

Of course the afternoon programming during the week is full of ads geared to the smarter sex (I hope my wife reads this). Clothing, hygiene, children's cold medicine, and the like bombard the viewer. Fortunately, I'm rarely in the position to be home at this time of the day, so I am not subjected to it. I have wondered, though, if any ads for monster truck rallies or World Wrestling Federation matches ever make it to the TV screen in the afternoon.

What really set me off, though, was an ad in one of my favorite wood working magazines. I do enjoy the normal array of tool ads and ads for books that are supposed to teach you 64,000 ways to router a door. I don't even mind the ads from the magazine itself telling me why I should subscribe to their magazine that I'm already a subscriber to. The ad that touched a chord, though, was a full page one showing a kindly white-haired gentleman bending over a table saw with a new hearing aid barely visible in his ear. The worker said something like his hearing aid was the best tool in this shop. I'm sorry, but I have a problem with this ad. First of all, while I am a fanatical woodworker, I am not white-haired, (some would tell you I'm not much of a gentleman, either). Also, not all people that love to play in sawdust are of the senior set. More importantly, no self-respecting woodworker would say the most important tool in his or her shop is a hearing aid. Maybe if the most important tool in this guy's shop was hearing protection, he wouldn't need the hearing aid in the first place. After taking a pen out and drawing a moustache, beard and tattoo that simple said "Mom" on the guy in the ad, I felt better and went on to look for an ad for a miracle saw blade.

Maybe I'm just being too hard on advertisers, but I'm sure we all have seen ads that raised our blood pressure or just made us shake our head. I am glad, though, that I have yet to see any hygiene product ads in my woodworking magazines, so I guess I ought to be thankful.

And that's the situation as I survey it…

"$3000 Toilet Seat"

I wish furnaces lasted forever. No, I haven't been keeping my head too close to the propane tank on the barbecue, but I can tell you every time something wears out, it snowballs into something else. Earlier this year, my family reminded me that not only was our furnace 35 years old, but our home doesn't have central air and they weren't happy about the thought of going through another hot summer surviving only with fans.

My formal training requires me to not simply launch into a new infrastructure purchase, but to ask if there were other home items we should be considering along with this one. So a family meeting was held with a new furnace and central air at the top of the agenda. After a long discussion with me coming up on the short end, I thought perhaps there was something to be said for dictatorships. I soon discovered that we didn't have enough storage space and a separate guest room/sewing room would be a nice addition. Ah! An addition. That could be the answer. We could add on to our house, install a new and larger furnace with central air and our needs would be satisfied...or so I thought.

An architect was contacted and schematics were prepared. It was going to be lovely, I hoped. Confidently, I called another family meeting (you think I would have learned...). We reviewed the work. It was lovely my family said, but some new concern developed. Considering the cost to add on, maybe we should be looking for a new and larger home with ALL the features we were looking for. "Drat", I said to myself. "I think I've created a monster". So off to our friendly realtor we went. After scouring the ads, the books and the signs we decided to once again convene the family to see where we were.

A new twist raised its head at this meeting. Since we were talking about finding a home with exactly what we wanted, why not consider building our dream home. After wrestling the samurai sword out of my hands, my family convinced me that the idea has merit. So here we are today, knee deep in home plan books and vacant land listings in search of the perfect combination. I'm not sure we will ever find it, and we may stay put, but I can't help but think how much not putting in a new furnace could cost me.

I should have remembered the story my father-in-law tells about the $3000 toilet seat. No, he doesn't work for the federal government, but he did get a new toilet seat for Christmas one year. It seems that before he could install it, a number of items had to be changed to make it just right. Well, $3000 later the new toilet seat was bolted down next to the new vanity, new tub, new fixtures, etc…and looked just fine. I think if someone tries to give me a toilet seat for Christmas I'm going to lose it in the wrapping paper.

And that's the situation as I survey it…

"Kids Can Be Great"

I was talking to my daughter the other day....you might remember her...I've talked about her before....she's 12 ½ (going on 32). Anyway, her mother mentioned to me she was running for Student Council at her school. When I asked Katie how the campaign was going she told me she won the election. I couldn't have been more proud. I started to tell her that I had been on student council when I was in school and, as a matter of fact, was elected President of the council my senior year in high school. She simply gave me "the look" and reminded me that my high school alma matter wasn't very large and then muttered something about everyone being related. I didn't care she was slamming my beloved Bessemer SpeedBoys, I was still smiling about *her* victory.

I think all parents are like that. We want the best for our kids and love to share in their triumphs. It's especially satisfying when they follow close to your own interests. I've always enjoyed the political process. I am continually fascinated by government and I'm very fortunate that my profession allows me to work closely with many government officials. I now have to wonder if my daughter has some of the same interest in politics. Long before this year's general election, together we watched the Minnesota Gubernatorial debate on C–Span. I was surprised Katie sat with me and watched since there was no music video involved and she has never been to Minnesota. After the debate was over, she said she was impressed with what Jessie "The Body" Ventura had to say. She went on to say he was the only one that sounded sincere. I kind of felt the same way, but I was sure conventional politics would prevail and Jessie didn't stand a chance. Well, I was definitely wrong. It seems a majority of the people in the land of 10,000 lakes felt just as Katie did and soon Jessie will be moving into the Governor's mansion. Katie was on target with that prediction.

Our son, Matt, on the other hand is not much of a political pundant, but he sure gets wrapped up in numbers. He loves to torment his parents by announcing how far off each of the clocks in the house is from the "real" time. This information is always followed up with some shortcut to victory on the latest video game he mastered. Neither of these pieces of information is especially useful to his parents, but we usually endure the delivery and try to get him to move on to something else. Matt is my outdoor buddy. Even though he is a little short of 10 years, he knows how to melt his old man's heart by talking about how he can't wait to reach the age when he can go with me back home to the UP to go hunting. He even mentioned the other day, he thought he would like to go to Michigan Tech after high school and become an engineer. Since it says Michigan Tech on my diploma I was pretty pleased to hear it. Being a degreed Surveyor, I will have to work on his choice of majors, but I've got time.

I know Ellen and I are blessed to have the two kids we do. We always try to remember that especially when the note comes home from the teacher that mentions someone got his name on the blackboard for not being as good of a classroom citizen as he could have been or when the local library leaves a message that a certain book is overdue and it's somewhere in the abyss of a young lady's locker at school. I'm sure those traits come from their mother (*grin*)...

And that's the situation as I survey it...

"Millennium"

I don't know if I can survive the rest of the year. Here we are only slightly into 1999 and already I want to start screaming. I think you know why. It's not because of my kids (although my blood pressure rises occasionally). It's not because of my job (even after attending my seventh night meeting in four days.) It's not because of my Harley...it could *never* be my Harley. My upset has been caused by one word...*Millennium!!!* This is like a bad dream or the OJ trial (which may have been one in the same) and the worst thing is that it is just beginning.

Usually toward the end of any year we have to endure the normal "Year in Review" garbage that spews all over everything. The "Best Dressed" and the "Worst Dressed". The ten greatest news stories (usually none have happy endings) and the rise and fall of various celebrities like Leonardo what's-his-face. Typically, this barrage lasts a few weeks and it's over, leaving us to get back to our normal lifestyle, but I have this knot in my stomach that we are going to have to deal with an entire year of comparative drivel about this century. Am I really going to be able to relate to the 100 most interesting people of our century? I have a hard enough time relating to those for last year.

Of course the biggest topic has been and will be those dreaded three initials...Y2K. That's right, the year 2000 bug. We have all heard about it. It is the condition where at 12:01 am January 1st, 2000, the entire world will halt. All computers will shut down because they won't be able to recognize the year 2000. Commerce will be crippled and we'll be reduced to hunting our own food and cooking over an open fire...as my daughter says, "yeah, right!" Companies that specialize in solving these Y2K problems have sprung up overnight. For a generous sum of cash they will come in and tell how big of a crash you are going to have and for slightly more cash they try to fix it. Personally, I think the fixes can cause bigger problems than the cure.

For example, when I came back into my office the other day, I noticed a big, fluorescent green sticker on my computer announcing that my 'puter was "Year 2000 Authorized". After breathing a sigh of relief knowing that I was going to be able to continue to pound out these columns without bringing down the free world around my knees, I went about my business. It only took about 71/2 minutes, though, to feel my blood pressure rise. It seems whatever was done to make my innocent little PC Y2K compliant now prevented me from doing several very important functions that I was able to do only a short time prior. After working on the problem for the rest of the day, my company's computer expert told me the bad news was that he hadn't figured out the problem yet, but the good news was I was lucky to have a big green sticker on my computer "cause now I was ready for January 1, 2000." I felt so lucky I tore the sticker off my computer and put it on his...maybe he'll feel as "lucky" as I do when the cure creates bigger problems than Y2K disease on his machine. I then proceeded to take out a pen and pad of paper. I'm pretty sure the New Year won't hurt that too much.

And that's the situation as I survey it...

"House Building"

I never realized just how many different selections of wallpaper there are. If you are like me and thought maybe a couple of hundred, you wouldn't have even been close. In the last several months, I must have gone through at least that many wallpaper books with a hundred different sheets in each book. You might be wondering at this point about my choice of reading material. No, our local library still has a great selection of best sellers and I didn't stumble onto a great deal at a rummage sale. Actually, my wife and I have taken a big plunge......we have entered into the head banging, gut wrenching, marriage testing, financial crippling arena of new home construction. Lock your doors and hide the small children because it has begun.

Most of our friends show big encouraging smiles when they hear the news and say things to us like, "Wow, that's great!" or "It sounds wonderful". But I know when we're not around they say, "Boy, we really thought John and Ellen made a great couple. We're sure going to miss them together." It seems that building a new house is supposed to be a death sentence passed on to your marriage. Now Ellen and I aren't newlyweds, although it feels that way (I threw that in because my wife proof reads my articles and with all this house stuff it couldn't hurt, right?). Although we have our share of tension, we usually work pretty well together. Our kids can testify to that....no, wait a minute, don't ask the kids. But this house stuff is something new. I have heard that even the most solid relationships develop a few cracks going through this process. Personally, I think all of these negative comments have historically been generated by people like Liz Taylor or Zsa Zsa Gabor as an excuse to dump spouse number 14. In fact,

I'm not so sure that in ancient times if you wanted to get rid of your significant other you simply convinced them to start building a new cave and then used it as an excuse to have a little "accident" and pretty soon you were out swinging a club for someone else.

Well, as the song goes "it's too late to turn back now". Contracts have been signed, the bank has gleefully agreed to a number that puts a knot in my stomach, and the home that we have worked so hard to get just the way we wanted it has a for sale sign out front. By now you have to be appropriately questioning our sanity, but let me assure you we are very sane (twitch, twitch). We just found the house we're currently living in wasn't *exactly* what we needed and we couldn't find what we wanted on the existing home market, so here we are.....knee deep in wallpaper books and fabric samples. Personally, my bride and I have an agreement. I handle all the details of what is going inside my woodshop and she handles everything else. I think that's fair and it really limits any debate. A friend asked if I was nervous about what she might pick and I responded, "How could I.....she picked me, didn't she?" My friend kind of mumbled something about a poor example, but I didn't quite understand it.

I hope we can keep our sense of humor through all of this. I believe that if we can, it will be the key to a successful project without having Judge Judy dividing the assets. Besides, what would Ellen do without me....there wouldn't be anyone around to put the woodshop together.

And that's the situation as I survey it...

"The Battle with Age"

I may not be a kid anymore, but I sure don't think I'm old. I have turned the big 40 this year and all of a sudden, things have taken on a different perspective. I don't think I've changed that much, it seems to be the people around me that have. I hear way too much conversation about hair loss (mine is a little thinner, but still quite dark... thank you very much) and low fat diets. I usually hear this about the time I'm unwrapping a "Poptart" or asking the waitress if they have anything besides chicken on the menu. I'm sorry, unlike most adults today, I can't quote my exact cholesterol number (Doc says he would like it just a little lower) and I thought triglyceride was one of the main characters from Jurassic Park. Today, I listen to my peers talk about swinging a club, when they used to talk about going to a club.

When this kind of "old guy" talk really gets to me, I bring things back into focus by calling or emailing my lifelong friends buried deep in the west end of Da U.P. They put things back on track. Where I grew up, the only one that knows anything about cholesterol is a lab tech and you can still engage 5 different guys at the same time about which is better....an Arctic Cat or a Ski-Do. I don't think anyone has ever won that argument, but I don't care, it always makes me feel good to hear it. Messages deal with going to camp, weekend hunting trips, and the latest town gossip (yeah, men do that too). I can always count on the "guys" to remind me how important it is to have the right outlook and fight the battle of age not with grace, but kicking and screaming. That is, until recently.

This spring, my brother, my cousin, and a couple of my friends decided to venture below the bridge in search of the elusive turkey. The only wild turkey back home comes in a bottle, so they decided to apply for a "troll" hunt (people in the U.P. call folks that live in the Lower Peninsula "trolls" because they live "below the bridge"). Now, I couldn't pass up an opportunity to meet my buddies and get a quick dose of attitude adjustment, so we made arrangements to meet in the middle of the mitten. As I was traveling to meet them, I couldn't help but anticipate the laughs and the jokes and the stories I was going to hear. I knew I would take a little razzing because I still live with the trolls, but that's ok, it would be worth it just to get my batteries recharged.

We arranged to meet at a rest area and I couldn't hide my smile as I saw their truck approach. My smile turned a little crooked, though, when I saw my cousin get out from behind the wheel wearing a new pair of glasses. I immediately asked him about the new specks and he admitted age was catching up with him and he finally broke down and started wearing them. Then he started talking about bi-focals like I was supposed to know all the latest advancements. To make matters worse, one of the other guys was eating a cookie out of a bag clearly marked "low fat". I thought to myself, "If anyone mentions their cholesterol level, I'm going to deck 'em." Fortunately, the conversation got back to the one I wanted to hear. I heard the plans for the hunt, all about the last trip to the camp, and of course, the latest gossip. When I left them to head back farther into troll country, I felt fully recharged. I didn't feel 40. I felt more like 20 again and it felt great. As I thought about the afternoon, I couldn't help but admit perhaps we can't avoid growing a little older, but you have to fight it all the way, so I tuned the car radio to a rock station, turned up the volume, and jammed all the way home. It took two days for my ears to stop ringing. I guess I'm not as young as I used to be.

And that's the situation as I survey it...

"Vacations"

The sun is shining. The water is warm. The kids are home. This can only mean one thing (no, not that there is a bussing strike). It must mean its *summertime* and summertime means vacations. By the time this is published, I will have already taken one short vacation. A quick trip with my wife and young ones to their Grandma Becky's house for the Fourth of July. You see Grandma Becky lives in the heart of one of the most parade walkin, sparkler flyin, flag wavin, domino droppin, potato sack racin Fourth of July celebrations that exists today. People come from all over to help celebrate the anniversary of our great country's independence. I will have eaten way too much barbeque, dropped countless ice cream cones on my shirt, and no doubt have developed a pretty good sunburn from watching all the parades without any sunblock. It is all worth it, though, because my hometown has been celebrating like that since there has been a town and it makes me smile to watch my kids get as excited about being there as I am. My mother works as hard with her grandkids as she did with my siblings and me to make just the right costume for the kiddie parade. Whether it's a monkey suit or pooh bear honey pot, you can be sure that one of her grand kids will place in the money for the best costume. Of course, all that participate get something, so everyone is a winner.

Since there is still some summer left, I have been planning a couple more vacations. Nothing real long in time, but enough to break away from the normal routine. I think at the end of the month I'm going to head to our neighboring state to the south and take a woodworking vacation. I know I have you scratching your head and you are wondering if my dust mask has been too loose, but seriously, there is a small shop in northeastern Ohio that holds regular woodworking classes on a variety of subjects. Now to make this a complete trip, I'm going to travel down on my Harley. That way I can kill two birds with one stone. I will have a great mode of transportation to see the countryside and will take part in a great class to learn some new woodworking techniques. I only hope we don't build anything too big as it will look pretty strange strapped to the back of my wide glide.

Of course, more vacation time will have to be used when the big day comes....you know....THE DAY. The day the builder, township, and banker say we can move into our new home. I'm so excited; I can leave fiber out of my diet. So how is it coming you ask? Well, let's see. Ellen and I are still married (and still speaking to each other). The builder says we are still on schedule and we have officially closed on the house we have been living in for the past 6 years. Looks to me like something's going to happen whether we like it or not. I guess you are going to have to stay tuned to see how it all turns out. But if you see me on the side of the road holding a sign that says "I will work for a place to sleep" you will know something went haywire. As you travel out on your own vacations this summer, keep me in mind, especially if you need a house sitter. We may have a heck of a deal for you.

And that's the situation as I survey it...

"Move In Day"

There are certain things in life that can make your stomach start churning. For example, when you look in your rear view mirror and see the overhead lights of a police car behind you. Whether you are the one he stops or not it usually makes your heart jump. Another example would be opening the front door to greet your daughter's date only to find someone standing in front of you with blue spiked hair and 17 earrings. He may turn out to be the nicest young man you ever met, but until you get to know him, you probably will have to reach for the antacids (or maybe a big rock...). To me, another one of those Mylanta moments is when you decide to build a new house. If you have been following the saga of my family and I, you know a little over 6 months ago the hole was dug for the foundation for our new home. Well, I'm happy to report we moved into our new house on August 19th, about 6 months and 2 weeks from when the hole was first dug. There is a mountain of boxes to dig through and I'm still trying to figure out which light switch turns on what light, but we're in. While my stomach churned a few times during the last 6 months, as with most things, it wasn't as bad as it could have been or as some people have described it.

Ellen and I are still married (I might even add the word happily, although you may want to confirm that with her...) and we are now enjoying setting up the new house the way we want it. I know we are very lucky, but it took a lot of effort as well. We worked hard together in the beginning to plan what we wanted. We asked thousands of questions of anyone that would listen and read anything that we could to help us identify potential problems along the way. We had good builders with good subcontractors who we now consider our friends. Even the movers added to the success as they did an excellent job. We all worked as a team to get the things done that needed to happen to make this dream become a reality. As with anything so involved, there were a few bumps in the road, but we tried to take them all in stride and focus on the bigger picture. Overall it was a lot of fun to see the work take the shape of something we have wanted for a long time and if I have my way (which usually isn't the case) we will be here for a long time.

Even though in the past I told myself I would never build a house, I have to admit I am very pleased with the results. I guess the lesson I learned is that you shouldn't always be nervous about what appears on the surface, but work hard to understand the entire picture. I don't think we will be looking at new house plans anytime soon, but who knows what the future will bring. I may have to build again just to get away from the guy at the front door with the blue spiked hair and 17 earrings....although a big rock may be less hassle....

And that's the situation as I survey it...

"Eating Crow"

I friend of mine told me once that his mouth was only a storage place for his foot. The more I think about it, the more I believe he is right. I have tasted shoe leather on more than one occasion and something in my system doesn't seem to learn from the experience. Once, at a social function, I commented to one of the folks that it was nice he could bring his daughter. Imagine my surprise when it turned out to be his new wife. How was I supposed to know about his mid-life crisis? The taste of leather remained in my mouth for several days.

Even though I know you should be careful about using words like always or never, they seem to continually crop up in my vocabulary. Of course, that's when I end up with foot and mouth disease. One of the best examples of this has me currently eating crow over a column I wrote a couple of years ago where I took aim at the game of golf. I remember writing more than a few negative comments about the sport and those who played it. Well, break out the breath mints because it's time for a retraction. I have to admit I have been bitten by the golf bug. I started the year in my usual way, getting on the course only when I had to support some charity, but all of a sudden I found myself enjoying the darn thing. I started playing every week or so and now I find myself on the course whenever I can find a good excuse. I bought my first golf sweater (which raised a few eyebrows at home) and while traveling recently, I even bought a golf magazine. It said it could cure my slice, but it hasn't. I don't care. I enjoyed reading it all the same. I have met some of the nicest people while playing golf and even though I'm still pretty bad, I'm getting a little better. This is encouraging to me and keeps me wanting to come back to the course. My daughter found me the other day watching an infomercial on some new multi-metal kryptonite shafted driver and thought I had lost my senses. I told her I was ok, but I sure had the taste of leather in my mouth.

I read somewhere that it takes a big man to admit when he's wrong. If that's the case, I have to be one of the biggest guys around because I find myself being wrong more than right. It's all right though, because I have found something I enjoy and hope to be able to do it for a long time to come. Now if the course would only let me use my Harley as a golf cart, I could combine two things I enjoy very much.

And that's the situation as I survey it...

"Post Millennium"

Well, the fact that I'm pounding out this column on my computer is the telltale sign that we've all survived the millennium. Not only did we survive it, we did it in such a quiet fashion, it was almost boring. I must confess that my family and I did very little in preparation for the stroke of midnight on January 1, 2000. We did fill up a couple milk jugs with drinking water and I had my kids fill the bathtubs around 10:00pm on New Year's Eve. I only did that in case something did happen, I wouldn't have to dig a hole outside and put up a Yooper guest house. With women at home that are used to modern conveniences, I didn't want to chance it. Besides, our subdivision rules don't allow detached structures and I don't want to rile up my neighbors by making them look at a little building with a half-moon carved on the door. My wife and I didn't let anything else bother us as we ushered in the new century with 450 of our closest friends at one of the parties in the area. It was a wonderful time that was made even better when at midnight the band was able to keep playing and the ice machine kept my drinks cold.

The next day I searched high and low in the paper for remnants of any disaster that would lend any credibility to all the pre New Year baloney that I had to endure. Low and behold the biggest story of the day was that there were no disasters. In fact, most agencies that were charged with keeping us from falling off the end of the earth (it is flat, you know) reported one of the quietest nights on record. Water was flowing from the taps, electricity was flowing from the outlets, and money was flowing from the ATM machine (which certainly made the retailers smile since the paper was also loaded with after New Year sales fliers). Since then, I did read where a young man in Oregon returned an overdue video and the store's computer spit out a bill for over $91,000.00. The quick thinking clerk actually grabbed a pencil (of all things) and a calendar and corrected the amount. Another potential Y2K disaster was averted!!

I hope as we proceed through this next century we spend a little less time looking for ways to be recipients of gloom and doom and more ways to enjoy everything that is right with the world. I have to believe many people learned a hard lesson that when we pull together we can still overcome darn near any obstacle thrown our way. Either that or they just like the taste of freeze dried food, storing gasoline by the barrel, and building their very own Yooper guest house.

And that's the situation as I survey it…

"March Madness"

I know by the time this gets printed, it won't be March anymore, but I couldn't resist writing about a pretty special month. It's not just special because it's the month of my mother-in-law's birthday (that ought to get me a couple of brownie points). It is special because I think March makes the male of the species think of their roots more than any other month. The reason for this is "March Madness". It's the rite of the college basketball tournament. I believe it annually causes us to think about not only our favorite colleges, but also our old high schools as we scan the paper for the results of district and regional match-ups. While this trait certainly isn't limited to just men, I have a hard time imagining the NCAA playoffs make the agenda too many times when the fairer sex get together by themselves.

Every school in the state gets gripped by playoff fever and usually the main topic of discussion is the chance of victory in the next match-up. I also enjoy listening to the war stories of the past. Every school has them. Whether it's the upsets of their arch rival; the high school players that went on to be stand outs in college, or even the guys good enough to play pro ball. Usually, these stories are also accompanied by other exploits of the past such as the time several of my fellow classmates and friends skipped school to have a smelt fry after beating our high school arch rival the night before. The party didn't last very long as it only took the principal about 20 minutes to figure out what was going on when he received the attendance report for the day and only half as much time to track everyone down. Over the phone, he rationally explained the need to return to class to further their education. Actually, I think his exact words were, "You all have exactly 10 minutes to get back to class or the doctor will be picking splinters out of your $#@% for a month from riding the bench so long." Even though it happened about 25 years ago, that story still gets dragged out about every March and in a warped way is now a fond memory.

I guess we wouldn't be so interested in this ritual if we didn't feel so strongly about our hometowns or alma matters. I was at a conference earlier this year when I ran into a great guy who not only grew up in my hometown, but now lives in the same place I do some 550 miles from where we were both raised. Along with some others, we spent quite a while comparing notes on our buddies from back home as well as some of the great moments in Bessemer Speedboy sports history (don't laugh, it really is our school's team name). We had a great time trading stories, but one thing was very clear: the strong connection with our roots was still present. It is the same with the people I work with. During the NCAA free for all, I hear more college stories than the rest of the year combined and almost always with the strong allegiance for the university that they wrote their checks to.

I'm not sure I care who wins the tournament that occurs in March, but I am glad they are being played. Without them, I know a little part of the ties we have may diminish, but as long as "March Madness" comes around every year the stories of the exploits of the Bessemer Speedboys will continue to be told.

And that's the situation as I survey it...

"Evening Meetings"

In my business there are a number of joys. Being a part of projects that go from the idea board to the drawing board (or computer screen as the case may be) to the ribbon cutting ceremony, provides a great feeling of satisfaction. Being able to work with folks from all walks of life as they support their community by providing direction and input makes the job a rewarding one. One of the negatives, though, is the fact that most of the committees, commissions and councils meet in the evening. Also, it seems that as your stock rises in a community the demand for your time also increases. Whether it's the public works board, planning commission, city council or township board, the weekly evening calendar seems to become a solid black line. There exists a running joke in my office that if we had a nickel for every time we have to recite the Pledge of Allegiance, we could retire early.

Evening events outside of your career become a luxury and you can never make personal plans too far in advance because different groups may request your presence with little notice. But there is typically one night that you can call your own. That is the fifth of any particular day i.e...the fifth Monday. Because of their scarcity, the evening of a fifth Monday is like a holiday. Dinner reservations can be made in advance, soccer games can be attended or (god forbid) lawns can be mowed. The evening of a fifth Monday is like waking up thinking it's time to get ready for work and finding out it's only 3:30 a.m. and you can go back to sleep for a while. Sometimes you simply do things on the fifth Monday that you normally can't do, such as watch the first half of Monday Night Football without the aid of video tape.

However lately there's been an infringement on the sacred fifths. It seems the secret of no regularly scheduled meetings has leaked out and these beloved holiday evenings have become the night to shore up lagging committees or to hold specialized public input get-togethers. This practice has to be nipped in the bud. Perhaps Congress should convene a special hearing on the matter prior to considering a legislative effort to ensure sanctuary from meetings on the fifth of any day of the week. Surely our sanity would warrant this type of consideration or, with my luck, the hearing will be held on the 31st of the month.

I guess I'll just have to grin and bear it. Besides, the nickels I'm putting away for each meeting are really starting to build up. I don't have enough for retirement, yet, but don't tell Ellen about the new chrome on my Harley. It might affect the allowance she gives me....but that's another story.

And that's the situation as I survey it...

"Family Golf"

I think I just discovered one of the greatest things about taking up golf. It's a game the whole family can get into. Both of my kids and my wife have taken lessons this year and have found the time to get out on the course and spray some balls. In fact, I'm not sure I haven't created some monsters. I remember coming home from work one evening only to see a new pull cart in the garage alongside a new pair of golf shoes. I knew they weren't for me, since they were about half the size of the snowshoes I wear. My wife told me, after my eleven year old son Matt finished his first junior golf outing, he just had to have some new equipment. Fortunately, I was already able to borrow some junior clubs, so I didn't have to spring for a new oversized head, graphite shafted, square grooved, info-mercial hawked set...or at least so I hoped.

I thought it would be cool to take Matt out one evening when the course is typically quieter and he and I could do some father-son bonding and hit a few balls. Unfortunately, the junior golf program had just handed out rule books and Matt had read it cover to cover. Now, even though I have only been seriously golfing a year or so myself, I know the standard rules of the game, but can't recite the rule number. Well, Matt could. And when he wasn't telling me about every rule he could remember, whether it applied or not, he was telling me about the fact he needed a lob wedge and that's why his game wasn't up to par. Don't get me wrong, we had a great time and he hit some great shots. I simply had to stop him occasionally and tell him to take a breath. He is sure fun to watch, though. He has a great swing (I wish I had one like his) and no doubt will be kicking my backside in a year or two.

I also enjoy playing golf with my daughter Katie and my wife Ellen. They are real troopers. It is a great feeling to watch them step and hit a good ball and even when it's not the best, they still want to play more (at least most times). We have met some very nice folks while golfing together and there is no doubt what we will be doing as a family unit on vacations from now on. Katie can really handle a golf cart. She says it is good practice for when she turns 16. I don't really want to think about that yet. It is just a lot of fun spending time with her while I can still control her driving.

I know my family is hooked when I hear more talk around the supper table about playing golf than anything else. There is even an occasional joke. Matt came home from junior golf just the other day and announced he had heard a new joke on the golf course he wanted to share. I quickly thought about the last joke I had heard on the course and shuddered. I hoped it wasn't the same joke for his sake and mine. I told him it was ok to tell it and he went on to say... Moses and Jesus and an older looking man were playing golf together. They came up to a long par five with a big pond about 200 yards from the tee. Moses teed up the ball and drove it right into the water. Jesus stepped up after him, teed up his ball, and did the same thing as Moses. He drove his ball into the water. Both Moses and Jesus were surprised to see the older man pull his driver out of his bag and tee up his ball. Since they both drove their balls in the water, they thought for sure the old man would not try to drive his ball over the pond. The man, with kind of a crooked stance brought his club back and with a little grunt he hit the ball. It was heading in the same direction as the first two balls that were hit. Moses looked over at Jesus with an "I told you so" look. Just as the ball was about to hit the water, a frog jumped up, grabbed the ball in his mouth, and began to hop on dry land. The frog didn't hop 5 times before a bird swooped down and picked the frog up with the golf ball still in his mouth. The bird flew across the pond over toward the green. It circled 4 times around the green and dropped the frog. As the frog landed on the green, the golf ball came out of his mouth and rolled across the green around the flag and into the hole for a hole in one. The old man simply smiled as he replaced his driver in his bag. Moses looked over at Jesus and said, "Man, I hate playing golf with your Dad!!"

I laughed pretty hard when Matt told that story, but was probably happier that he has found a comfort zone in something he likes to do. Everyone should have something they do as a family and I'm glad we are working on ours. I'm just not sure I'm going to be real happy when I have to ask them all for strokes.

And that's the situation as I survey it...

"Bad Habits"

I'm not exactly sure when this is going to be published, but by the time you read this, I will have either just celebrated or will be about to celebrate my 18th wedding anniversary. I know an 18th anniversary doesn't hold a candle to the 50th or 70th anniversaries I read about, but I'm pretty happy to be at 18 and still counting.

I was thinking about the changes in both of our lives in the last 18 years and couldn't help but smile. I'm sure you would agree that most of our adult behavior has its roots in early family life. Since you meet your spouse typically after developing your habits, it's not unusual for a few things to clash. Naturally, our mates will try to soften some of the rougher edges or change a few of the bad habits. I tend to blame all my bad habits on my upbringing (especially when I get caught), but that doesn't hold any water with Ellen. She contends I'm an adult and shouldn't do some of the things I still do. She isn't totally innocent herself and I've been working on changing a few habits of hers as well. I know we have both been successful in making improvements in each other, but Ellen would tell you her list for me was and is a lot longer.

I learned the basics pretty early in our marriage such as putting the seat down and throwing my dirty clothes in the hamper. When I was single, I didn't own a hamper and come to think of it, didn't have many dirty clothes either (at least that I defined as dirty). To my credit, I did teach Ellen how to cook quickly after we got married. Before a fry pan comes flying out of the sky, let me explain. I taught Ellen everything doesn't have to be cooked until it is classified as a building material. I also taught her no matter what the food situation is around the world, you don't have to clean your plate. If you are full or don't like broccoli, you don't have to eat it!!! I still hear childhood stories on how to hide food from Ellen's brothers and sisters.

Ellen is working hard to get me to stop incorrectly using the word "bring". For some reason, my Yooper DNA has programmed me to say, "Bring this to your mother" instead of "Take this to your mother". She really gives me a ribbing when I slip up, but I guess I deserve it. I was also brought up eating cereal out of Corning Ware bowls and potato chips out of Tupperware bowls. For some reason, Ellen grew up doing the exact opposite. I don't fight her on this very often, but if I want to get her goat a little bit, I'll get a big plastic bowl of chips as a late night snack and sit down in front of her and eat them while watching TV. When I'm finished, I'll turn to her and ask her to bring the bowl back to the kitchen for me. Then I usually duck because I know I'm going to get it.

It's been a lot of fun spending the last 18 years with my bride. We have had a few downs, but luckily, mostly ups. Ellen has really had the tougher job of breaking me of my bad habits. My list has to be 10 times longer than hers, but I'm working on it. I'm not sure what the next years together will bring, but maybe over time, I will finally learn which bowl to use for cereal.

And that's the situation as I survey it...

"School Behavior"

I've been out of school a long time, but recently had to venture back for the annual parent-teacher conferences. I'm never very comfortable doing this because it brings back some unnerving memories of when the conferences were about my performance in school. I was usually able to pull reasonable grades so that didn't worry me. What did was mother's usual remark as she headed out the door on her way to my school. She would look at me and say, "I'm going to make sure Mrs. So and So knows if you act up, not only does she have my permission to give you what for, but if I find out you'll get it again." These aren't real comforting thoughts for a young lad who was known to shake the authority tree every now and again. So, I would have to hold my breath until she got home to see if the teacher squealed on me about any bad behavior. It's kind of funny that I never seemed to remember my mother's warning before I was about to commit the crime, but always seemed to remember it after I got caught. My teachers were actually very understanding and usually if I caught heck from them, they didn't feel the need to tell my parents. My mother generally would come back home and report to my father that I had a good report card with "ok" citizenship. I would let out a sigh of relief and tell myself I should work harder to stay out of trouble. A little voice inside of me would be quiet for a second and then I would hear it say, "Nah!"

Fortunately, I don't have as many of the same concerns with my own kids (they must take after their mother) and I enjoy meeting their teachers. They are extremely dedicated professionals and you can tell how much they care about their students. They usually have good things to say about my offspring's behavior even though I know they aren't always angels. I believe, though, they behave a little better than I used to. Also, the modern terms used by their teachers are a little softer. Some of my old teachers would say a student disrupted class; today they call it being "a little too social". In my day, you may have been labeled a "trouble-maker". Today, you may hear, "has some difficulty respecting authority". I probably wouldn't have been as nervous if I knew all my mother was going to hear was, "has some trouble keeping with the school code". I know I would have breathed easier sooner.

Even though I may have found myself on the wrong side of the line every now and again while in school, I did try to work hard. Also, for the most part, I did behave. It was usually pretty easy until that little voice inside of me started making suggestions. Then, I guess I became a little "too social" or had some "difficulty in keeping with the school code". I hope my mother doesn't read this. She still remembers the good reports, but always tells me I'm never too old to get "what for" from her.

And that's the situation as I survey it...

"Johnny Big Time"

I remember growing up listening to an AM radio station with my father. It wasn't that I was particularly fond of AM radio, it simply happened to be the only station available near my hometown to listen to. It wasn't all that bad. It had a mix of local events, music, news, sports, and of course "trade-eo". Trade-eo is a program where you could call in and tell the announcer that you had something to sell and he would put you on the air so you could describe it and give your phone number out to prospective buyers. It was cheaper than a classified ad and probably reached a lot more people.

One of the songs that I remember listening to during those years was an old country song that had a major theme of "Some days are diamonds and some days are coal". No matter how many years pass and how many things go right, I still remember that song as I watch certain days in my life turn and go south. Most of those days I can laugh about later, but some stick pretty close. I try not to drag those up from the depths of my memory too often. Usually, the ones I can laugh about are the ones that go south on a visit back home. It seems no matter what good things happen in my life, I have found my friends and family back home have a way of bringing me back to reality.

Earlier this fall, I attended a meeting of a committee I belong to on the campus of Michigan Tech. This meeting happens twice a year and since Michigan Tech is only about 100 miles from where I grew up, I usually get a chance to head to my hometown for the weekend and visit with my family and friends. This particular meeting was over in the late afternoon and I jumped in my car and headed for Bessemer. I received a message from one of my brothers that he and several friends were heading to camp for the weekend and I should head directly there. I had a big smile on my face as I traveled the quiet back roads to get to camp.

My smile faded quickly, though, as I reached my destination. I had thought I would get to camp ahead of everyone else, but unfortunately, the camp was full. Normally, this would be a good thing, but I had committed a major error. Because I thought I would be at camp before anyone else, I hadn't changed my clothes after my meeting. I was about to walk into a camp full of Yoopers wearing a suit and tie. I broke into a cold sweat as I headed for the door. My only chance was to rush inside directly to the bunk room and change as quickly as possible. I thought that would minimize the view and therefore minimize the harassment. I was wrong. I no sooner hit the door when the place went dead quiet and all eyes turned from the card table to me. I mumbled a couple of feeble "howyadoin, eh" and tried to sneak out of sight. As I was changing I heard someone say, "Who was dat?" Someone else answered "I think that was Johnny Tie-Man". "No" someone else said. "It was Johnny Below-da-Bridge". After the laughter died down, someone else asked, "Now what is he doing?" and I heard an answer of "Probably pulling the tags off his new camp clothes from Cabelas". Again, I had to wait for the laughter to die down before I could go back into the main room of the cabin and wait for an opportunity to put someone else in the hot seat. That certainly was the beginning of a "coal" evening, but it did get better and I can laugh about it now.

Things rolled along pretty well the rest of the fall (I even had a couple of diamond days) until deer season and my trek back home to spend deer season at the camp. This time I showed up wearing the proper gear (wool pants and a red and black checked jacket). What I didn't know was an article had found its way in the local paper about an award I had received earlier in the year. To make matters worse, the article had an old picture of me accompanying it. Much to my dismay, when I walked into camp, someone had cut out a copy of the article and picture from the paper and taped it to a piece of poster board. Above the article was written in large letters "Caption Contest". There were already several entries written on the poster board and as deer season progressed and more people visited the camp, the entries got quite large in number and quite clever. I think the cleverness was in proportion to the number of libations that may have been consumed while visiting camp. A couple of my personal favorites include, "Hey, Chico! Where's the man?" and "I didn't know Saddam Hussein was a surveyor". I took it all in stride and looked for an opportunity to get a few digs back when I could.

One of my friends told me later one evening at camp, I wouldn't get picked on if they didn't care about me and "Besides," he said, "We only get to see you a few times a year. The rest of these yahoos we can pick on anytime we want." I guess he was right. I'm going to be a lot more careful the next time I head "above da bridge", but just in case, I hope I have a few more diamond days, before getting hit with more lumps of coal.

And that's the situation as I survey it…

"Yooper Movie"

Before the next person asks, No, I haven't seen "Escanaba in Da Moonlight". I'm not sure I'm going to either. I still bleed Yooper blood and there are several reasons I may not ever see it. I remember after watching "Fargo" a few years ago, how sorry I felt for anyone from either of the Dakotas. It seemed as though everyone I talked to couldn't resist saying "Oh jeeze, Marge" at least fifty times. If you want to go even farther back, there was a movie in the mid-eighties that featured a beer drinking pair of brothers from Canada. After this movie premiered, I had to spend almost a year listening to "Take off, eh. You Hoser." Even my wife's family thought it was hilarious that our young niece called me "Uncle Hoser". I'm not sure I want to subject myself to another dose of supposed entertainment at the UP's expense.

My wife did see the play and came home just shaking her head. Bear in mind she has been keeping company with a native son of the UP for almost twenty years, so she kind of qualifies as an expert. She said the story line wasn't too bad, but did note no one spoke the real Yooper dialect. When she told me two of the main characters were named Jimmers and Reuben, I knew I would have a hard time going to see either the play or the movie. You see, I grew up with a Jimmers and a Reuben and I'm not sure any play or movie could do their lives proper justice. I'm sure for those of you that have seen the movie or the play you are simply thinking there is no way real life could be as far out as this story. That may be, but I'll let you be the judge. You see, the Jimmers I grew up with was known to be a little off kilter at times. For example, there was the time he made his way into our town's storm sewer system and kept popping up in the downtown area speaking to shoppers from the catch basins. He scared the heck out of a number of senior citizens who weren't sure where the voice was coming from. I also remember one instance when Jimmers decided to have a birthday party for his lawn mower. I was home from college at the time and was sitting in Jimmers' rented house high on a hill near the south edge of town with a number of other guys that were simply killing time (or brain cells) on a hot summers' night. When Jimmers mentioned the idea of a party for his lawn mower no one objected. Who were we to question the actual birthday of his yard maintenance equipment? So we sang a slurred version of "Happy Birthday" and poured a couple of cans of refreshment over the guest of honor. Jimmers then decided to give his mower a present and started it up in the middle of the living room and proceeded to run over that day's newspaper. The mower must have liked it, because it never missed a beat as it threw paper shreds all over the house. We all got a big laugh out of it and Jimmers got a visit from the local constable investigating a noise complaint. When he saw who was living in the house, the constable simply shook his head as he knew Jimmers pretty well and this episode was fairly low on his crazy scale. I could go into a lot of other events, but I think you get the picture and I would rather not incriminate myself.

So, when someone asks if I have seen the "Yooper movie", my usual response is, "No, I don't have to see it, I've lived it. Then I quietly start humming "Happy Birthday to you" as a smile comes across my face.

And that's the situation as I survey it...

"Male Bonding"

I was listening to a comedian the other night on TV who was commenting on the fact that his girlfriend couldn't go anywhere (including the restroom) without having a friend come along. He then went on to say that men were different. I did a lot of thinking about that and I have to tell you I disagree. I think men are more like this comedian's girlfriend than we care to admit. We simply call it something different and find it in different places. Men call this need to be together "fellowship" or "camaraderie" and we are always finding excuses to be together in many ways and in different places.

It may start right at home when a group of men gather in the living room to watch a football game. It doesn't take long before they are high-fiving each other and talking about their own glory days playing high school sports. It may take place at church where there are always men's groups formed to do good work for their congregation. It may also take place at a local service club where men can get together and not only provide great community support, but also huddle together to tease a fellow member or listen to the latest town tale (If you don't think men gossip, you probably were searching for your present from the Easter bunny a while ago). On the more seasonal side, one of the largest "fellowship" gatherings of the year is the annual trek to the North Country in search of the elusive whitetail. Where else can you go and see men cook meals fit for a king, sit around a fire and tell the tales of the woods that would make even the heartiest of woodsmen look over his shoulder. Sometimes it's cold, sometimes it's wet, but each year it's a given that we men will get together to share some time in the woods.

Even though I participate in all of the above methods of bonding with my fellow man, one of my favorites is spending time at my golf club. This is one of the greatest places for male bonding that ever existed. It is full of guys that share the same passion as I do, to hit the little white ball into a hole that in my opinion needs to be a lot larger to help my game. We get a chance to meet each other on the course and really get to know each other after a round of golf while sharing a meal and something cold and refreshing. Whenever I walk into my club I see numerous smiles on the faces of the staff and most of the members. Occasionally, someone may not be too happy with their game that day, but the good news is tomorrow is another day and we get to try it again. Whether you are a great golfer or just a duffer (like me) you have the opportunity to play a round of golf with just about anyone you would like to. My wife, kids and I can spend some quality time together at our club and I will have those memories forever, but I will also cherish many from the times the "guys" get together. There I always find the good shots and the not-so-good ones, the jokes and the stories. The people like LB and Slash who, along with many others always make me feel at home. The matches and friendly wagers are all part of this ritual we call male bonding and I'm glad I can be a part of it.

This is why I think that comedian was wrong. Men may not want to admit it, but we need to be around each other as much as the ladies. Just don't ask a man to go to the restroom with you.

And that's the situation as I survey it…

"Getting Older"

I know I'm getting older, but I don't feel old. I feel about the same as I did when I was 18, except I might have a few more aches and little less hair. There are definite signs, though, that tell me I am getting "longer in the tooth". One is I find myself reading the obituaries in the local papers as well as the paper from my hometown. I don't have any particular explanation for doing this, but for some reason I have to turn to that section each day. I read my hometown paper via the internet and skip right over the births section to see if I recognize anyone in the obits. I can't remember exactly when I started to do this, but it is something I simply do now as a matter of habit. Another sign of advancing age is I just celebrated my 20th anniversary with my company. Twenty years!!! Heck, it seems like yesterday I was pulling into the parking lot of my company behind the wheel of my '69 Buick LaSabre packed with worldly possessions. They included a box of books, my new college diploma, a suitcase, a black and white TV, and a stereo complete with an 8 track player (don't laugh, it was paid for). I wasn't sure what this Yooper was getting into, but I was ready to give it a try. Of course, it also means I will be celebrating my 19th wedding anniversary this year. I'm sure that hasn't aged me at all (I threw that in so there will be a 20th wedding anniversary). Still, as I look back, I guess a lot of time has gone by.

I believe one of the biggest reasons people age, but don't feel old, are their kids. I know it may not sound logical, but let's think about it. As parents, we age a little every time they do something; their first steps, learning how to ride a bike and their first day of school, to mention a few. They make you feel young and alive when they come home and show you how they learned to write their name or read you a story they wrote. Or when they sit down after dinner with you and try to convince you to buy them a stereo using the logic that it will free up room in the house because they will be in their own room listening to their music. My daughter is currently taking Drivers-Ed which is another reason to feel a little older, but also a little more alive. I have taken her out a couple of times to practice and she does a pretty good job. While I'm very nervous about her on the road, I'm proud of how alert and observant she is and how hard she is working on getting comfortable behind the wheel. If I remember my own days of drivers' training, I had already been driving for quite a while (someone had to drive during bird season) and the very first day of class I was marked down for "palming" the wheel going around the corner and for asking the instructor if we could cruise down Main Street to see who was hanging out. I'm sure I will feel a little older when Katie gets her license, but I am enjoying her learning what it's all about.

I guess I simply have to accept the fact that I am not 18 anymore, no matter how good I feel. Actually, I don't think I'm ready to give in just yet. In fact, I think I'll jump on the Harley and cruise down Main Street to see who's hanging out.

And that's the situation as I survey it...

"9-11"

This being the fall, I have the occasion to jump in my vehicle periodically and head north to my homeland to see if I can recharge my batteries a little. The trip is a long one. It covers about 550 miles, two time zones, three great lakes, and you never leave the state. I have made the trip with any number of people, in all different types of vehicles, in all kinds of weather, but usually in the fall it is made by me, myself and I. I don't mind making the trip by myself as it gives me a lot of time to think and plan and reflect. The first trip this fall was especially reflective given it was only a few days after the national tragedy that took place on September 11, 2001. I'm not a particularly emotional person, but I have to admit I shed more than a few tears as I was winding down the road listening to "I'm Proud to be an American" on the radio and looking at all the American flags flying on homes, businesses and passing cars. I have heard that song a thousand times if I have heard it once and it has always made my eyes water whether we have been in a tragic situation or not. I have never really understood why I felt that way until a little later in the trip.

I arrived at my mother's house in the middle of the day and went in to say hi and make sure all was right in her world. We chatted for a while and I got caught up on all the latest happenings around town. It was a beautiful early fall day, but my mind kept wandering and I found myself staring out the window instead of paying attention to the lovely lady that brought me into this world. I apologized for rushing off, but I wanted to catch up with my brother and cousin to find out the game plan for going to camp later in the day. When I did catch up with everyone, I found out they all had things to do in the afternoon and weren't going to be at camp until the early evening. I decided I would get the weekend's shopping done and head out to the woods by myself until the rest could break free. I arrived at camp, got it all opened up, put the groceries away and sat out on the deck with the sun in my face and had one of the most calming moments in my life. I thought about the families affected by this tragedy and how we all had to pull together to get through it. I thought about how I felt when I lost my father almost 6 years earlier. I miss him a lot, especially this time of year.

During the various hunting seasons in the fall and winter, Dad spent most of his free time giving us life's lessons and teaching us values whether we knew it or not. I'm not sure even he knew what he had done, but the more I thought about everything he taught me, the better I felt. It simply hit me while I was sitting there. He was just like most fathers, giving his family the best he could in every way. I realized it is our job to not only put those teachings to good use, but to pass them on to our own family. I also realized the reason I feel the way I do about that song and this country. It is exactly how my father taught me to feel and judging from the closeness this country feels now, it's apparent my father wasn't the only one who taught his children to feel this way. I *am* proud to be an American. I am proud of the feelings my father instilled in me and I am going to work hard to teach my own children to feel the same way. We need to pass this on to all our children as our fathers have done. I knew I was right about this when a couple of hours later my younger brother showed up at camp and the first thing he did was put up an American flag. I guess Dad did a pretty good job.

And that's the situation as I survey it...

"New Technology"

The advances in technology we are exposed to everyday never fail to amaze me. As I sit here at my computer looking at a screen that is less than 4" deep, I can't help but think back to the first computer my company ever purchased. It was an Apple and when it arrived, you would have thought the President of the United States came to the office. The new addition sat in a very prominent spot where everyone could see it and I remember the terror in the eyes of our bookkeeper as she had to learn to how to do our payroll using that box of circuits. She had been our bookkeeper for a long time before we got the computer and in her estimation had gotten along just fine without one and didn't see why we needed it in the first place. In fact, she confessed to me later, for a number of years she kept a duplicate written set of records, because she didn't trust the darn thing anyway. Oh, how times have changed. It wasn't all that many years later when this same bookkeeper came into my office fairly frazzled to let me know our entire accounting department was unable to do "anything" because our computer network was down. I had to smile as the visual of the first day she sat down at the Apple came into my mind.

Fear of technology certainly isn't a new thing. I recall my father telling a story about his mother and her first exposure to technology. My grandfather had purchased the first radio the family had ever owned and turned it on early in the morning to listen to it before heading off to the mine. When he left the house, he didn't turn it off and my grandmother was so scared of it, she wouldn't go near it and although she didn't want it on, she didn't know how to turn it off so it played all day until my grandfather returned home from work that night.

One of the places where I really see changes is at one of the most remote locations of wilderness survival....deer camp. You wouldn't believe how things have changed. The days of men huddled around an AM radio sitting on a table in the middle of the room being lit by a white gas lantern and heated by a pot belly wood stove are pretty much gone. Today, it's a TV (usually color), a generator, cell phones, a propane furnace, walkie-talkies, GPS units (to find your way back to camp), and the first item on the grocery list is AA batteries. I guess we have come a long way from white gas lanterns and wood stoves.

Sometimes we think we can handle technology when we really don't understand it. Since my youngest brother doesn't read my writings, I guess it would be ok to tell a story about one of his experiences. As I understand it, our local bank back home had just put in a drive-through system that was one of the first in the area. My youngest brother was heading to the bank to cash his paycheck when he decided to try out the bank's newest technological feature. He pulled up alongside the system and smiled as he endorsed his check, placed it in the system and hit the send button. What he didn't realize was that he was supposed to put his check in the plastic carrier before sending it up the line. He simply placed his check in the chute and sent it on its merry way. The teller came on the intercom and asked how she could help him and he told her he would like to cash his check. She said that would be fine and to send it to her. I can't help but imagine the looks on both of their faces when he said he already had sent it and she realized what he had done and now this check was floating somewhere in their maze of tubes. If you knew my brother, you would know he watches his money pretty close and didn't like the idea of his paycheck stuck somewhere between he and the teller. As the story goes, with a whole lot of emotion and a little luck the bank was able to retrieve the check relatively intact and finally cashed it for my brother. I believe the next day large signs went up explaining the proper use of the drive through banking system to their customers. I think my brother changed banks (just kidding).

I guess we will never stop being exposed to new technology and I have to believe the vast majority will be extremely beneficial to our lives. Although, I'm pretty sure when the bank comes up with a "star-trek" like transport system to cash paychecks, I'll bet my youngest brother won't be at the front of the line to try it out.

And that's the situation as I survey it...

"Protestors"

I was in Washington, D.C. recently when I had one of those memory flashbacks that don't occur very often, but when they do it can raise the hairs up on the back of your neck. I am fortunate to have visited D.C. several times and have always enjoyed the history surrounding our Nation's capitol. This time was a little more trying, though, as a large number of demonstrators had moved into town. I'm not exactly sure what the demonstration was about, but I know both sides were represented and it really messed up the normal flow in town for a couple of days. I was talking with several folks from the local area and they made it sound as though this was a pretty regular occurrence as people tend to use Washington as the focal point for their issues. It made sense to me, but I couldn't help wonder if the regularity of these types of actions don't lessen their impact. It certainly seemed to with the local folks as they simply shrugged and knew it was going to take them a little longer to get home.

The whole situation brought back the vision of a couple of demonstrations I orchestrated in my youth. No, these weren't anything elaborate (I was only 6 at the time), but I do remember their result. If memory serves me correctly, I was unhappy about something my father did or wouldn't do for me. I wasn't sure what to do about it until, while watching TV, I saw some news footage about a demonstration somewhere in the world. I saw hundreds of people waving signs and getting a lot of attention. I figured if it worked for them, it might work for me. I rummaged around until I found a piece of paper and a crayon. I didn't have a stick, but I did have a piece of string. So in big letters I wrote "Daddy is Mean" on a piece of paper and taped the sign to the string and hung it around my neck. I then proceeded to the sun porch where my father was reading the newspaper after having a "not so great" day (I found out later). I started to march back and forth across the floor of the sun porch until he put the paper down to see what all the noise was about. If I would have waited a little longer while I was watching TV, I may have seen the part of the news story where the police showed up and "persuaded" the demonstrators to move their demonstration elsewhere. I may not have seen that part on TV, but I can assure you that in a not so small way, I experienced it. Before I could utter one chant, I felt a hand on the back of my collar and I felt my feet leave the ground and I was mysteriously moving through space. I could see the back door ahead and felt myself being propelled into the back yard. I didn't land real hard but for some reason, my backside hurt like you know what. I then heard "the voice" and it said, "I can show you mean if you would like me to." I might have been young, but I wasn't slow and had heard that tone enough to know that any answer was going to be the wrong one so I decided silence was best. I didn't move until I heard the back door slam and I knew it was safe to get up.

Being a headstrong young man (thickheaded some would say), it wasn't long before I forgot about the result of my demonstration. Another issue arose and I felt the need to take up a cause once again. This time my father didn't have such a bad day and instead of doing anything he simply ignored me. As much as I marched, the more I flashed the sign, the less attention he gave. After a little while I got tired and abandoned my crusade for a favorite cartoon on the tube. I don't know if I got involved in a demonstration ever again. I thought a lot about the memory as I watched the demonstrations in D.C. and how little it seemed to matter to the people it was supposed to directly affect. In about two days without any fanfare, the people who had jammed the streets quietly left. With the exception of some litter, you wouldn't know anyone had been there. I guess sometimes the best reaction is no reaction and the situation will take care of itself. The right of expression is very important, but I guess so is the right to ignore and my backside for one was very happy with the latter.

And that's the situation as I survey it...

"Gadget Boy"

My wife really enjoys teasing me about my interest in technology. She knows I graduated from Michigan *Technological* University, not some basket weaving university, yet she always shakes her head when she sees me watching a program about the latest gadget. In fact, whenever she wants to poke fun at me, she'll just smile and call me "GB". This, of course, stands for "gadget-boy" and I seem to get called "GB" a lot. I have to admit gadgets catch my attention, but I don't think I'm a gadget junkie.

I have to be careful, though, whenever I head back to my homeland in the wilds of the far western end of Michigan's Upper Peninsula. For the most part, things up there don't evolve real fast and people don't like to change unless there is a pretty darn good reason to accept it. I remember a year or so ago I went to camp in the fall to do some bird hunting. We headed into town for a few groceries and I volunteered to drive. On the way, someone asked what the blue button was on my dashboard. I explained it was a way to connect to a service that could help you if you needed it. "Like, how?" he asked. I said I would show him and I pushed the button. After a few seconds a friendly voice came on the speaker and said, "Hello, Mr. Matonich. What can we do for you today?" As a demonstration, I asked him for directions to the store where we were going. He not only told us how to get there, but exactly where we were. My buddies in the vehicle were pretty impressed except they said it wasn't a whole lot of help since we knew where we were going, anyway, and certainly knew where we were at the time. To try again to prove the point, I locked the doors while we were still driving and called the service back. I told them my doors were locked and could they unlock them for me please. Sure enough, a few seconds later there was a click and the doors unlocked by themselves. The boys jumped a little, but still weren't really impressed because as one of them said it wouldn't be of any help to him since he never locked his doors anyway. I quit while I was behind and drove the rest of the way to the store without even setting the cruise control.

OK, maybe I am a "gadget-boy". I like my voice activated cell phone. I carry my lap top computer everywhere (except camp). I have the latest digital readout on my wide belt sander in my wood shop and I'm trying to lower my golf scores by using the latest swing trainer. My son isn't any better. Not only do I have to listen to him tell me about the latest electronic features of just about anything, but now that he is old enough to hunt, he is on top of any new advancement in the firearms and hunting industries and gives me every good reason why he should have it. My buddies at camp always say the apple doesn't fall too far from the tree.

Even though they might not recognize it, there seems to be more "gadget-boys" back home lately. When I was at camp this past deer season, I noticed a lot more hand-held global positioning system (GPS directional) units on belts and walkie-talkies appeared to be pretty popular. It seemed everyone had a cell phone. We're even discussing a color ac/dc TV with a remote control for camp. I almost fell off my chair one evening when I actually saw one of my buddies pull a *laptop computer* out of a case and plug it in while the generator was running so its battery would charge. I guess even Upper Peninsula deer camps have caught the technology bug. I was going to ask my buddies why the sudden interest in GPS since they claim they always know where they are and where they're going, but I didn't want to stop the technological momentum now that it's started. Besides, I kind of like the idea of a color TV at camp. Maybe we could even think about a satellite dish next year. It would sure make those Packer football games come in clearer and I'll bet I could program the remote to...ah....well...never mind....

And that's the situation as I survey it...

"Memories"

I was undertaking one of my favorite pastimes the other day, raiding the fridge, when I saw a fresh basket of tomatoes on the counter. I stopped and felt my mouth start to water. It had been a while since I had a good tomato and I really wanted one. You wouldn't think it was a big deal to go ahead and eat one, but my stomach hasn't been able to handle a fresh tomato in a long time. So, rather than eat it and suffer through the night, I let my mind wander back to many years ago when eating a fresh tomato was a very common occurrence.

When my father was alive, he prided himself on having the best garden in town. He worked from dawn until dark in his garden and while it wasn't very large, I have to admit people came from all over town to admire the quality of the veggies in Poncho's garden. When I was a kid, it seemed I spent my entire youth picking rock, weeding, watering, and pulling weeds in that plot of ground and hated every minute of it. That is until the time came to be able to eat the season's efforts. I can remember pulling two fresh tomatoes off the vine and handing one to my Dad and we would then sit down across from each other at the picnic table in the backyard. He would take a salt shaker out of his back pocket, take a bite out of his treat, pour salt over the wound, and hand the shaker to me. I would repeat exactly what I had just witnessed and we would sit in silence eating our tomatoes thinking about what we accomplished that year and what was in store for us during the next growing season. Eventually, the conversation would start and we would talk about a lot of things past, present, and future. You've read a lot about "life's simple pleasures" and in my mind this certainly qualifies.

My love of fresh vegetables wasn't confined to just our garden as several of my friends and I would wander around after nightfall and look for other gardens that may have things to share. The owners of those gardens weren't necessarily ready to share the fruits of their labor which is why we did it at night. We occasionally would find ourselves staring at a flashlight beam and what looked like a gun barrel. No one ever took a shot at us (well, almost no one), but we did get caught every now and then, and would have to spend a week working in their garden to make up for the mischief we caused. We swore we'd never do it again, but until our interests turned in a different direction (still soft and fresh, but you didn't have to wait for the fall to go looking for it) we continued to check out the town's garden crop. Another one of life's simple pleasures.

You probably don't believe this all came to mind by simply looking at a basket of store bought tomatoes, but it did. I would bet that everyone has memories of those simple pleasures that get triggered by simply seeing or hearing something else. Maybe watching someone walking their small child triggers your own fond memories of walks with your own kids when they were young. Maybe a certain song on the radio comes on and you can't help but flash back to another place in time. I will bet you smiled as the song played and if you were alone, you probably sang along.

In these turbulent times, we need to focus more on life's simple pleasures. Not necessarily remembering times past, but creating memories today we can use in the future. I know I'm going to try. In fact, I just went to see my doctor who thinks thirty years of not being able to eat a fresh tomato is a little much, so he has put me on some new medication that so far makes me think my son and I will soon be sitting down together at the picnic table with a couple of red juicy tomatoes, a shaker of salt, and the opportunity to create our own simple pleasures. I do think I'll keep the stories about my evening exploits as a young man to myself, though, for a little while longer.

And that's the situation as I survey it...

"Million Dollar Shot"

I want to ask the question, "What has been your most embarrassing moment?" I've had so many I can't tell you which one is the worst, but I did have one not too long ago that ranks right up there. I had the pleasure of being asked to play in a three-day golf tournament with some good friends and great guys. I had never played the course before and asked if we could get a practice round in the day before the tournament started. My buddies told me it would be no problem and I would get a good feel for the course after the round.

A little less than a week before we were supposed to play, I was told there would be a "slight" change of plans. Instead of playing a practice round at the course hosting the tournament, we were going to make a detour to another course in a different town to play in a one day charity tournament. I didn't mind the detour. It sounded like a lot of fun and usually those charity tournaments are pretty relaxing because there isn't much pressure.

Our team actually played pretty well and I was pleased with my own play. I was able to contribute on some holes and actually was the closest to the pin on one hole of all the players in the tournament. On another hole I was able to make a long putt that got my team the lowest score on that hole of all the teams. Needless to say, when we got back in the clubhouse we were having a good time and really enjoying the day.

About then, it started to turn for yours truly. Since we had finished playing, I had put my clubs and various accessories away and sat with my teammates and enjoyed some liquid refreshment before dinner was to be served. I had forgotten there was one more contest that day and it was a very important one. Four lucky players were each going to be able to take a single shot at making a hole-in-one. If one of the players happened to be successful, the lucky player would walk away with a cool *million* dollars. Our group immediately agreed if one of us were chosen and the shot went in the hole, we would split the money four ways. I never thought we would see a chance at the money, let alone make the shot. I was simply content to go back to our table conversation until I heard an announcer slaughter a name that was pretty close to mine. It appeared I was going to be one of the "lucky" four.

Back to the truck I went to put on my golf shoes, get the right club and mentally prepare myself for something I really didn't want to do. For some reason I felt like Charlie Brown being told by Lucy to go ahead and kick the ball. You knew Lucy was going to pull the ball away at the last minute and Charlie Brown was going to end up flat on his back. Charlie Brown knew this too, but had to try to kick the ball anyway. Like Charlie Brown, I knew I was going to try the shot.

One of my playing partners was kind enough to take me out to the spot where the shot was to occur. Thinking I needed time to prepare, he never said a word, but let me slowly sink into the reality of what I was about to do. I watched as the other three contestants stood up to their shots and proceeded to hit the ball forward, but were never close to the million-dollar prize.

Now it was my turn. All I really wanted to do was hit the ball. I didn't care if it even went close to the green as long as it went reasonably forward. I took my stance at the ball and took a practice swing. It was a very good swing and I could feel a little confidence come back to my system. I took a deep breath and felt the club go up. I then felt the club go back down and strike the ground. I saw the ball squirt about 35 yards on a diagonal away from the green. I also saw a huge piece of turf fly straight down the fairway toward the green and land closer to the green than my ball.

The shot was over. The money was still safe in the bank and I tried to make the best of it as I got back in the cart. My buddy, the chauffeur, again never said a word, but this time I swear I saw a very faint smirk on his face. When I got back to the clubhouse, my other playing partners said they were trying to watch my shot from near the green, but all of a sudden a big piece of sod flew from the earth and blocked the sun and they weren't able to see a thing. I let them have their fun (mainly because they did have something cool and refreshing waiting for me). We had dinner and a few more laughs (at my expense no less) and left to head to the big tournament.

I replayed the shot way too many times in my mind as we traveled to our destination, but by the time we arrived, I kind of shook it off and tried to put it in the "let's forget about" category. This worked for about 7 seconds which is exactly how long it took my playing partners to tell everyone they could about that afternoon. By the next morning, not only did all 160 players in the tournament hear about it, but so did everyone in the supper club (including the staff) where we relaxed in the evening. There were people who never swung a golf club in their lives coming up to me to ask if I would tell the story.

I knew it was all in fun and being the new guy to this group you have to expect some razzing. I really did enjoy the entire weekend and my hopes are that my buddies will forget about that afternoon. But something tells me it will be a story that's told around that tournament for a long time to come. How many times does someone get a chance to shoot for a million dollars? This is one guy that hopes once is enough.

And that's the situation as I survey it...

"Crosswords"

My kids are starting to give me some grief over my age. Actually, so is my bride, but she isn't too far behind me so she uses a little more discretion. There isn't one thing that gets them going, but all the little things. If they catch me holding a piece of mail out a little farther in front of me I get the "Isn't it time for glasses, Dad?" speech. Both of my kids have glasses, but even at my "advanced age" (according to them) I haven't needed them. I will admit the date box on my watch is a little harder to see and maybe I do hold a paper or two out a little farther these days, but I think I still see pretty well.

Another thing I get grief over at times is my choice of clothes. I may come home with a new shirt or tie and you can bet my daughter will roll her eyes. Now, I haven't resorted to plaid pants with striped shirts, yet, but I believe my daughter thinks what I pick out is almost as bad. She gets her sense of fashion critiquing from her mother. Ellen has spent more than 20 years trying to teach me how to dress. I used to hear questions such as, "You're not wearing that to work are you?" My response was typically, "No, I have some extra time so I thought I would throw a few changes of clothes on to see if they fit." After a while, I would simply get "the look" and I knew I had to turn around and try again. I used to tell her she should get some of those "Ger-animal" tags and my life would be a lot simpler. She didn't think that was very funny, but I'm not so sure she didn't consider the suggestion.

The latest to trigger the age thing is my recent interest in working the crossword puzzle in the newspaper. I've tried to keep this quiet, but I came home one evening, sat down in a quiet spot and began to go through the daily puzzle when my daughter saw me and began to question whether I was all right or not. She razzed me pretty good until I gave her "the look" and she exited stage left. I had the last laugh, though. I was working on a puzzle the other day when I got stuck on an answer and asked her help. Pretty soon the whole family was sitting around the kitchen table working on the puzzle and I couldn't help but laugh because they were all having fun.

So, maybe some of the things we tend to associate with aging are for younger folks as well. My family certainly enjoyed working on that puzzle together. It was like a board game, but everyone was on the same team. I don't think they're ready to stop giving me grief over my habits, but I'll probably continue to do what I do. In fact, maybe there is a pair of plaid pants out there with my name on them.

And that's the situation as I survey it...

"Random Acts"

When was the last time someone did something special for you? Maybe, more importantly, when was the last time you did something special for someone else? I'm sure you can think back to a number of times when you were younger and tried to cook breakfast for your mother (usually a disaster) or saved your money so you could get your dad a special present. As we grow older, our attentions turn toward the special people in our lives. I remember once cooking a meal for a girlfriend on one of our early dates and how much she raved about boiled chicken, pasta, and canned corn. Shortly after I married her (I chased her until she caught me), I had to go out of town and I still smile at the memory of how special that homecoming was.

Doing something special can certainly extend beyond your home. I'm very proud of the people I work with. A number of years ago, one of our staff members was diagnosed with cancer and the rest of our staff for several years contributed to his family in many ways. Unfortunately, he lost his battle a little while ago, but the support for the family continued. We were able to give his family a little financial boost that they were not expecting, but appreciated very much. It is extremely hard not to feel good about helping.

We hear stories from time to time about random acts of kindness. Every time I hear of one I remember when I was a recipient. I was about six years old and walked uptown to the local market to buy a bottle of pop with some money I had earned. I placed the bottle on the counter and began to dig for the coins when I discovered I was a little short. I must have lost some of the pennies I had in my shirt pocket. I really felt embarrassed and was about to put the pop back, when I heard the clerk say, "It's ok. The guy ahead of you took care of it." I looked up in time to see the back of a head walk out of the store. I tried to run out to thank him, but I never did catch up with him. It may have been only a few pennies, but it had a big impact on me. In a town where I knew everyone, I never found out who was so kind. I had the chance a few years later to be the benefactor and surprisingly it was the same situation in the same little market. I was in front of a very young lad who was trying to buy a bottle of pop. He didn't look as though he had enough money either, so you can believe how good it felt to hand the money to the clerk and disappear out the store's door. I certainly hope he remembers and returns the favor to someone else along the way.

A service club I belong to was selling raffle tickets for a 100th anniversary model of a Harley-Davidson. The tickets sold for $100 each and only 299 were to be sold. I happened to be out of town the day of the drawing so I was kind of anxious to find out if I had won the bike. No, I didn't win, but when I found out who did, I didn't care. The young gentleman whose ticket was drawn didn't even know his name was in the barrel. His girlfriend, as a surprise, bought the ticket for him. More significantly, he won't be able to ride it for a while as he's currently serving in the military stationed in Iraq. Now there's a kind of homecoming anyone would envy.

And that's the situation as I survey it…

"Dumb All Day"

Here in Michigan we have a number of traditions. It may be watching the Wolverines play their fall classic against that school in Columbus. It may be continually holding up your hand to give someone a geography lesson about the mitten, or trying to hold your hand in such a way to make it resemble the look of the Upper Peninsula. I guess once you start with the hand thing, you can't stop even if it is practically impossible to make your hand look like the UP. One of the oldest traditions, with an extremely large number of participants in Michigan has to be our whitetail deer season. It only runs about 16 days, but it can involve a large percentage of the male (and a lot of the female) population in the state.

Typically the one central theme revolving around deer season is "deer camp." Whether you are in the southern tier of counties or the extreme west end of the UP (where I hunt), camps spring up or are opened up for those 16 days to give shelter to those in search of the "Big Kahuna". Of course, you can't have a place where men gather that doesn't yield a tradition, event, or a story that will live on as long as that camp is around. Our deer camp is no different. The camp is as far west in Michigan as you can go (here is where we would normally try to insert the hand visual) and has not only yielded a fair number of deer, but stories and traditions as well. Not all of them can be put in print. I would be violating the rule of "what happens in camp, stays in camp", but I'm sure I can share a few without too much retribution from the rest of the group.

As with most camps someone assumes the role of camp cook and food is extremely abundant. I have seen and partaken in many of these lavish meals. If some of the wives knew how well these guys can cook, there may be a change of duties on the home front. Whether it's "rigs and ravs" with the boys from Rocky Creek for opening day supper or lamb chops at the "19th Hole", everybody usually eats pretty well. I'm not much of a cook, so I typically share the clean-up duties. It's a small price to pay for the great meals Scotty makes for us.

After the dinner dishes are put away, a libation or two may be consumed. This can lead to the things that make it a memorable trip. This year was no different. The day before the season opener, we had a fair amount of visitors from neighboring camps. One of the visitors asked Scotty to cut his hair. Scotty is not only our camp cook, but tends the sauna fire, handles any electrical needs we may have, as well as being pretty handy with the barber shears. The type of haircut he specializes in, though, is one you may see on a military base when looking at new recruits. That's the style our guest wanted so that's what he got. Well, this led to a few more folks wanting to get their hair cut as well. This included my brother, my cousin, and his son. Fortunately for me, I value my hair more than the need to conform to the rest of the group, so I declined the invitation for a similar cut.

There was a lot of laughter that night as the mirror got passed around, but it was pretty quiet the next day when we headed out in the early morning to our respective deer blinds. I saw heavier stocking hats being put on and heard a whole lot of grumbling about better judgment. A few days later my brother and I headed into town to take his wife out for lunch. I think my sister-in-law summed it up pretty well when she took one look at him and said with a shrug, "I guess when you wake up dumb...you're dumb all day." After I stopped laughing, I saw the wisdom in that statement and knew this would be one of those events that would live on in the memories of those who were there. In case certain people try to forget, we do have pictures and I'm sure they will make their way to one of the camp walls.

I've hunted well over 30 years, and of all the traditions and stories, none make me smile more than the tradition my son and I started this year. Later in the season, I took him back to camp to hunt deer with me for the first time. He and I rode the 9½ hour journey to camp together and talked about a lot of things. He even got me to listen to one of his rap CDs and I got him to listen to a classic rock station along the way. He was a successful hunter this year and I'll never forget on the way back to camp he hugged me and said, "Thanks Dad. I'll never forget this." All I could muster for a response was "You're welcome" but I was thinking, "Guess what son, neither will I."

And that's the situation as I survey it...

"High School Senior"

Things are just a little hectic around the Matonich household these days. Normally, I would be the root cause of the chaos, but not this time. My lovely bride isn't at the center. Even my 14-year-old son is just kind of plugging along, so it isn't him. No, I guess the new level of stress is attributable to my eldest, Katie. Now, before she reads this and starts getting that "fire" in her eyes, I have to admit she has good reason. She is finding herself on the downhill side of her high school career. That's right...she's a..a..a....GRADUATING SENIOR! I had to capitalize it because that's about the volume of the conversation around our house these days. I think it was Charles Dickens who wrote, "It was the best of times, it was the worst of times." He must have had a graduating senior, too, when he thought that up.

This IS a very exciting time in a lot of ways. Katie is in the middle of selecting a college. Her mother (my lovely bride) isn't really happy with me, though. I'm kind of a softie and I let Katie apply to something like 857 schools and, of course, she was accepted to pretty much all of them. Oddly enough, very few have the word "state" or "public" or "Tech" in them. They are all for the most part billing themselves as "the perfect place for a young adult to learn about life and develop their own way of contributing to human kind." To make matters worse, Katie, being the good researcher she is, would like to visit a bunch of them. So, off we're going to see who has the best program for her major...oh wait...she hasn't chosen one, yet. "Not to worry," say these fine places of higher education. "We'll help develop your child's field of interest as we go." I was uncomfortable with this approach until I spoke to parents of previously graduated seniors and they said this style of curriculum is actually quit common. I guess my technical background with the square corners makes me ask the question, but I feel better after discussing it with folks who have experience.

Even with all the stress, I have truly enjoyed being a part of this process although I may not always admit it. I get the opportunity to discuss (argue about) her choices and I even get to spend some time with her as we go on campus visits. We recently went over to the west side of the Lower Peninsula to visit one of her choices. I had a lot of fun with her on the trip. The campus was high on Katie's list before the visit, but she wasn't as enthusiastic about it afterward. I'm proud of her skills to quickly analyze the good and the bad in each of these visits, but I also agonize with her as she struggles with this decision. I guess that's what parents do. We would probably be more concerned if she didn't care, but we know she will eventually settle on the right school for her. In the meantime, we'll pack up the car and head in several necessary directions. Hopefully, this will give Katie all the information needed to make her choice. While on these trips, I have the benefit of listening to a whole new group of classic rock stations on the radio and even get to lecture my soon-to-be adult daughter on the evils of college life....'cause that's what Dads are supposed to do. I read it in the Dads' handbook they gave me when we brought Katie home from the hospital almost 18 years ago.

I know the day will come when she will call me on the phone and want me to talk some sense into her own daughter about her choices. I'll probably put on a crooked smile and simply remind Katie of her own experience. I hope she develops a better sense of humor by then because she will no doubt be the one to pick my nursing home.

And that's the situation as I survey it...

"Mascots"

What does a "Flivver", "Midget", "Milltowner", and "Hodag" all have in common? Chances are you have no clue. In fact, a year ago I could have added the name "Nimrod" to the list and you still wouldn't know, but today that may have given it away. For those who watch ESPN, you probably have recognized the reference to "Nimrod" and now know the references are all to school team names in Michigan's Upper Peninsula and Northern Wisconsin. While the names all have a meaning, those schools have existed in relative obscurity until someone from ESPN discovered the Watersmeet Nimrods and decided to make a commercial for their network featuring this sleepy little town in the west end of Da UP. Now, Nimrod mania has struck the sports world.

The two television spots feature not only the Watersmeet basketball team, but also one of their strongest and oldest fans singing their school song. So many people have taken an interest in this team; Jay Leno's Tonight Show flew the entire basketball team (along with the town's 81 year old patriarch) to Los Angeles to be on his show. The school system cannot keep up with the orders for "Nimrod" merchandise and it has been reported that CBS will soon be filming a documentary in the area. The reason for the sudden interest may surprise some, but not those folks who are fortunate enough to have grown up or currently live in this area. It is hometown pride. It may have come as a surprise to ESPN to see most of this little town turn out to watch a high school basketball game, but it has been this way since they built their first school and started playing sports before the start of the 20th century. Some may attribute it to the lack of other things to do, but I know it is a matter of pride and support for their community. This type of support is not limited to Watersmeet, but can be found in towns across the country. Pride in our community is still the fabric that holds us all together. When this feeling is strong, the community is successful. When this feeling diminishes, so does the community itself. There are countless examples of this in every state.

Whether you are from Kingsford, Michigan (home of the Flivvers), Hurley, Wisconsin (home of the Midgets), Marenisco, Michigan (home of the Milltowners), or Rhinelander, Wisconsin (home of the Hodags) their hometown pride has been and will always be present. Even my hometown is part of this history. In fact, if you have seen the ESPN commercials you may have noticed the team the Nimrods were playing was from my hometown, Bessemer, Michigan. You can tell their opponents are from Bessemer because of the Watersmeet chant to beat the "Speedboys" which is the name of the school team from my alma matter. We may not have the most common names for our school teams in this area, but I can guarantee the pride is as strong as it always was and will remain strong long after the TV crews leave town. I hope this is the situation where you live. If not, it's never too late to catch the "fever" of hometown pride. Go Speedboys!!!!

And that's the situation as I survey it...

"Da Da"

My wife was looking out the kitchen window the other morning and she saw a doe in our backyard. This isn't too unusual, but this particular doe had a shadow. Alongside was a relatively newborn fawn. Ellen said the fawn hopped around and nudged her mom and generally was happy to have the sun shining in her face. She said it was fascinating to watch the fawn follow her mother back into the swamp...oops...I mean "wetlands".

I found this event interesting for another reason. It made me remember when our daughter was just a little girl hopping around after her mother instead of graduating from high school. Since the doe and fawn came into our yard on graduation weekend, I couldn't help but let the memory tapes rewind and play a little of Katie's life for me.

Katie has always been a little of a "Jekyll and Hyde" child. When she was a baby, you couldn't get her to go to sleep for all the stars in the sky. I remember trying anything I could to get her to go to sleep and how frustrated I was until that little head would pop up in her crib, look at me with a smile and say, "Da Da." That would melt any frustration away and I would go back to the crib and start all over again to try to pat her back to sleep. Later in life she hasn't changed much. She is very head strong (gets that from her mother), but can be as sweet as the day is long (obviously from her Dad). Just recently she teamed up with her brother to surprise Ellen on her birthday. I checked in with my bride in the early afternoon to make sure her special day was going ok. She seemed a little depressed. When I asked her why, she said neither of our kids had wished her a happy birthday. I tried to cover for them and after finishing with Ellen, I called my son and read him the riot act. He didn't say much other than he would handle it. Late in the afternoon while my wife was golfing with her league, my daughter and son had roses delivered to her on the course while she was playing. They evidently had been planning this for quite a while and their mother was really happy. I was happy for two reasons. First, my kids actually took the initiative to do something nice for their mother and, second, I don't think I'm getting the bill.

Katie has really become a fine young woman and I can't help but be proud of her. Soon she will be off to college and even though you can say it will be ok, I know we'll miss her. As I watched her walk up the steps to get her diploma at her graduation ceremony, I really didn't hear them call her name, but I did see that little head pop up in the crib and I know I heard, "Da Da" one more time. I will always see Katie as my little girl, but I know she's ready to face all the challenges the world has to offer. She'll probably do it with a little bit of attitude (again, from her mother), but she will never miss an opportunity to make a difference. That's why her mother and I are so proud of her as I'm sure every parent is of their own children. Especially when they give you that innocent look that simply makes you remember the last time they called you "Da Da".

And that's the situation as I survey it...

"Real Winner"

Whenever I write this article, I try to relate it to something most people have experienced or probably will experience sometime in the future. I've always felt it draws the interest of the reader when they can identify with the subject. Well, this installment may be a little different. I'm going to write about an experience I recently went through that most people probably will never go through. My hopes would be that after reading this and giving it some thought, perhaps I can convince a few others to follow down the same path.

I'm not exactly sure why, but earlier this year I threw my hat in the political ring to run for a countywide office. I live in a relatively large county and even with low voter turnout I knew it would require between 22,000 & 25,000 votes to win. Well, after the smoke cleared and the votes were tallied I didn't quite make it. I lost by about 150 votes with over 42,000 cast. In the end, while I may have lost the election, I couldn't feel any more like a winner and I need to explain why.

When I asked a few close friends for their thoughts about my running for office, I was surprised at how quickly they responded with a resounding "absolutely"! I simply chalked it up to friends supporting friends. But as I worked my way across the county, I couldn't believe how that sentiment was shared by people I had just met. People from all walks of life made it a point to show their support. Some through volunteering to help, some by offering their expertise and some by donating money to support my effort. This was particularly amazing since many of the people I didn't know very well, but they didn't hesitate to attend a fund-raiser when asked. Some didn't wait to be asked, they simply sent a check with a note saying, "Good Luck."

On the campaign trail, you have a tendency to see fellow candidates quite regularly. I felt sorry for them as they had to listen to my attempt at explaining what I would like to accomplish at least a dozen times. But each time I did, those other candidates would applaud politely and take the time afterward to tell me how well they thought it went. Many of these folks are veteran office holders and I really enjoyed getting to know them. I've always felt I am a passionate person, but don't hold a candle to some of the people I was fortunate enough to meet. It was a great feeling to see the political process at work and how common ideals can bring folks together from all walks of life. While I ran on one particular party ticket, I was amazed at the number of people who told me they crossed over from their normal party to color in the circle next to my name.

Well even with all this support, in the wee hours of the morning, after the ballots were counted, I still fell short. I've heard losing an election described as being "kicked in the guts". I have to confess, I've been kicked in the guts before and losing actually felt a little worse. But, the next day I attended a breakfast with many of the county's candidates and was greeted as a winner, not as someone who had just lost. It only reaffirmed what a great process we have in the USA and how proud I am to be a part of it. I may have lost an election, but because I have won more friends and gotten to know so many more people, I would call it one big victory. It wasn't hard to do. I simply needed to try.

It definitely was a wonderful experience I wish more people would try as well. I know it would be as rewarding for them as it was for me. One of my fondest memories of the entire experience came shortly after the election while I was at my favorite watering hole. A very good friend of mine approached me, shook my hand and said, "Congratulations!" I kind of shrugged my shoulders and replied, "Thanks, but I lost!" Wally simply smiled and said, "I know. I think you're already too busy without that job. Now go home and take your wife up north for a few days." I laughed, but did what he said. After all, every good politician should listen to his supporters.

And that's the situation as I survey it...

"First Job"

When was the last time you thought about your first real job? Not the one where your dad gave you 2 bucks for cleaning out the garage or your mom paid you to cut the grass at your grandma's house, but one where you got a real paycheck. I think my first real job (besides the Sunday paper route) was working at Pricco's Bakery. This wasn't your typical bakery. We didn't make any doughnuts or sweet rolls. This bakery specialized in very good Italian bread products. The owners were Dante and Teeni Pricco. The two brothers learned the business from their mom and dad who brought over their skills from the old country. My job was to come in after school and run the home style bread through the slicer. Then I turned my attention to the freshly baked hard-crust Italian bread that simply needed to be bagged. I usually was able to get this done in about two hours or so and it happened six days a week. Friday was payday. Dante would reach in his pocket and hand me $16 for the past week's work. He usually slapped me on the back of the head after handing me the money and complained about the youth of today not being the same as the kids were when he was young.

I worked at the bakery for several years before taking a job at our local Ben Franklin store. The boost in pay was tremendous. I was getting a dollar an hour, but was also learning valuable lessons about dealing with the public. Many of these lessons have been carried over for years. It was also the first job where I actually received a paycheck with all the appropriate withholdings. I remember wanting to know who that "FICA" guy was and why he kept so much of what I earned.

The reason for this walk down memory lane is my 15 year old son recently started his first job with a real paycheck. If you ask him what he does he would tell you he works as a club attendant in the bag room of our local golf club. The folks who play golf there and at other golf clubs would give you the short version of this position as a "bag rat". Matt's job is to carry people's clubs wherever they would like them and clean the clubs when the golfers are done playing for the day. He also picks balls off the driving range, cleans up around the bag room and performs any other tasks the head pro or his assistants need done. All of these things need to be done with a smile and a hearty "yes, sir" or "yes, ma'am". Besides the fact you should always be polite (which is a big part of the job), this particular position can be the recipient of gratuities from satisfied customers which is a far cry from the slap on the head I used to get from Dante Pricco.

My son seemed to learn fairly early in this job that being polite pays off. He has also learned that the customer is always right. A friend of mine was finishing up his play for the day when Matt came up to him to get his clubs. Matt said, "Hello, Mr. Salay. How did you play today?" My friend responded, "Mr. Salay is my father. My name is Paul." Matt replied, "I know Mr. Salay, but we are supposed to call everyone by Mr., Mrs., or Ms." "I don't care what you've been told," replied Paul. "My name is not Mr. Salay. Now here's five bucks. Do a good job on my clubs, please." Matt replied, "No problem, *Paul*," as he tucked the five spot in his pocket. "I'll clean them the best they've ever been cleaned and I'll scrub the grips, too, *Paul*". Paul told me later his grips were, in fact, scrubbed about the best they had ever been. I had to smile as my guess is Matt learned a life lesson on dealing with the public. Hopefully, one he carries with him throughout his work career. Give the customer what he wants and make sure there is value to what you do. Combine those two and the only real problem you may ever have is how to keep that "FICA" guy from taking too much of your hard earned pay.

And that's the situation as I survey it...

"Poncho's Garden"

As I continue to mature (or age, as my kids point out), I'm finding certain events or different smells are triggering memories of times past. Recently, some friends and I embarked on a sausage making day. We used some ground meat from a previously successful hunt and a recipe my father received from an old family friend who had passed away many years ago. We used to make it often when I was growing up at home, but hadn't made it in a while. As soon as we mixed the spices together, I caught their smell and my mind flooded with memories of growing up around this old family friend. My Dad and I would go to his cottage almost every Sunday morning in the late spring and summer. Dad would help "Jimmy" with whatever projects he had going and I got to fish for Northern Pike off his dock. Besides almost always catching some nice fish, the highlight was at noon when we all came in and sat down to a big dinner of spaghetti and meatballs prepared by Jimmy's wife, Margaret. It was about the best spaghetti I've ever had. Both Jimmy and Margaret came to America from Italy and were very proud of their heritage, but even more proud to be Americans. I spent many hours listening to stories about their "old country" customs and traditions. It amazed me that simply smelling those spices again would trigger all that reflection. It certainly had been a long time since I thought about those days.

I guess simply getting older causes this kind of reflection as well. I'm finding this to be true when I gather with friends from back home, especially at camp. It seems at least one night is spent reliving some past events. Many of them are old favorites and get told every year. Occasionally, someone will come up with a new one that I haven't heard in a while or perhaps have never heard before. That was the case this year when I heard a story for the first time involving my father. In order to feed a growing family, my father not only had a garden behind our house, one year he received permission to plant a garden on a vacant city lot we didn't own. I think the reason Dad got permission was because the lot was severely overgrown and the owner knew my father wouldn't rest until the lot was cleared and the ground was ready for planting. My father took his gardening very seriously, but I know it was always a labor of love. He worked every day on this lot for several weeks before he could till the soil and plant it. He then spent all summer picking rock, weeding, and caring for the vegetables growing tall and strong.

It seems this once vacant lot was located on a route used by one of the local parish priests for his daily stroll around town. He couldn't help but watch the hard work and progress my Dad made on this garden spot. In the early fall, the fruits of his labor were ready to harvest and Dad had stepped back to admire the garden just as the priest walked by. "Poncho," the priest called to him, "You and the Lord certainly have a beautiful garden." My father hesitated for a moment and replied, "Thank you, Father, but you should have seen it when the Lord had it all by himself." It took a while for me to stop laughing because I know that was how my Dad would have handled the situation.

It was great to hear a new story that evening. When I asked the teller why I hadn't heard it before, he said a previously told tale jogged his memory and knocked the story loose. I'm glad it did and I know it won't be the last time it gets told. I guess maturing does have advantages. One of them certainly is being able to add to the many fond memories of times past.

And that's the situation as I survey it...

"Stereotypes"

Did you ever notice how wrong most stereotypes are? I don't particularly care for them in the first place, but they seem to be quite prevalent these days. One of them near and dear to my heart is the geographic stereotypes that exist in Michigan and other states. Living in the Flint area, I know all too well how bad national exposure can taint feelings. I am fortunate to get to travel at times and truly enjoy being able to meet different folks around the country. Typically when they ask where I live and I mention the Flint, Michigan area, I get the "I'm terribly sorry" look along with the sympathetic tilt of the head. I can explain our area's benefits until I'm blue in the face, but I still think they want to reach out and pat my hand in sympathy. You would think with this type of treatment, people in the Flint area would be more conscious of stereotyping other areas of the country, but it's not the case.

Recently, I was asked to make a presentation on a national committee I chair. The presentation was going to be made to a state organization's annual meeting. I've always appreciated these types of opportunities, as it gives me a chance to develop a relationship with folks from a new part of the country. When I mentioned this to a few friends, I got the same "look" I've seen before. It appears they couldn't appreciate my invitation to Fargo, North Dakota in February. Now before you start nodding your head in agreement, let's examine the facts. The weather is of no consequence to me. Having grown up in the far west end of Michigan's Upper Peninsula, cold and snow is a regular part of most weather forecasts there (even in the summer). Yes, I did see the movie "Fargo", but didn't get all the supposed humor. I didn't laugh much during the movie "Escanaba in Da Moonlight" either. I guess my roots explain that as well. I also know several good North Dakota natives and have never once heard them say, "Aww, jeeez, Marge". Even armed with these distinct realities, the folks from Flint who typically cringe at the mention of any movie with "Roger" in the title actually had me second guessing my own convictions.

To make matters worse, I found myself sitting next to a Fargo resident on the airplane flying in. She wasn't any better as she spent a good part of the flight telling me all the reasons she really didn't want to be heading back to her home. I was finally able to get her to tell me some attributes of that part of the state and found them to be very interesting. The metropolitan area surrounding Fargo has a population approaching 125,000 people. There are a number of educational institutions in the area and several major employers. She admitted her own business had all the work it could handle and the property values for residential housing were exploding. Quite a far cry from a mental picture of a barren wasteland with 40 mph winds and 6 foot snow drifts.

After I landed, I continued to see why the area was doing well. The people I had the opportunity to meet were tremendous hosts and great folks. I got to spend a fair amount of time with them and never once felt like an outsider. In fact, when I called my wife the next day to let her know I arrived in one piece, she asked how I liked being there. I answered it was just like being home. Since she travels back to the UP with me quite regularly she knew what this meant.

The bottom line is no matter where you are or where you're from, you should find the good things about the area to focus on. Believe me, if people live there, you can bank on some good things happening around you. Attitude is the key and it is definitely infectious whether positive or negative. For me, I'd rather have it be positive. Even the good folks in my native Upper Peninsula keep the faith. Just remember, "Say Ya to Da UP, eh!"

And that's the situation as I survey it…

"New Driver"

It is kind of an exciting time at the Matonich household, yet there is a little anxiety in the air as well. The reason is our youngest is about to turn 16 and that can only mean one thing….a shiny new driver's license. Our son, Matt, as any other normal, soon to be sixteen year old, has been waiting for this for awhile. As I was driving home from work the other day, I was thinking back to the days when I was in the same boat. It was a different time then. I learned how to drive pretty early in life. My Dad and I spent so much time in the woods; my mother felt better knowing I could drive in case there was a problem. I even bought an old VW before I was 16 to use on our bird hunting trips. But none of that meant anything when it was the time to make it official.

I remember making an appointment on the day of my actual birthday and showing up about two hours early. I had been practicing the various maneuvers for a month and even though I had been driving for about 5 years (I told you I started early), I was still very nervous. I guess all the practice paid off because I walked out of the Secretary of State's office with a license in hand. I was very relieved, especially considering I had sold my old VW and bought a nice used Chevy pick-up in anticipation of getting a license. Needless to say, I burned a couple of tanks of gas that night simply riding up and down the main street of my hometown. There were no FM stations (or FM radios for that matter) to be found in those days and the only decent AM station was WLS out of Chicago some 400 miles away, but it played the kind of music my buddies and I liked to listen to and they boosted their signal at night so even we could pick it up. None of us could afford an 8-track player. We could barely afford gas, so it was a long distance AM station that kept us company. The $1 an hour I made at the local Ben Franklin was barely enough to keep gas in the tank and the insurance paid.

Of course, another thing that comes with owning an older vehicle was the need to know how to keep it running. From the simple oil changes to new plugs & points (if you can remember what those are) to major engine and transmission work. You either learned how to do it yourself or you found a buddy who could. I still have most of my tools and was pretty handy around a vehicle from that era. Today is another story. All you have to do is open the hood and you can pretty much guarantee it's going into the shop for repairs. Matt may think he is lucky not having to know how to do this kind of work, but I think he is missing a great part of growing up. Greasy fingernails and bloody knuckles were badges of honor. Being able to make an engine sing was a great feeling. Learning how *not* to fix a rust spot was just as important as learning the proper way to fix one.

Matt and I were discussing his first vehicle the other day and I was pretty happy to hear what he was interested in. I'm sure a "vette" would suit him fine, but he sounds like he wants to follow in the old man's footsteps as he would like to look at older pick-ups. I can guarantee it will have more than an AM radio and more than likely not have any rust, but maybe I can find one with standard transmission so he can learn what it is like to use a clutch. In fact, maybe there is a red '69 Chevy pickup out there with three on the tree and an AM radio with his name on it.

And that's the situation as I survey it…

"Time Savers"

As I was driving home from the office the other day, I was thinking of how many different routes I've used in an attempt to shave a few minutes off the trip. It seems, like many others, I'm caught up in the race to save time. I believe a lot of folks are even obsessed with it. You might even say I'm one of them. With that said, though, I'm not really sure all this hi-tech gadgetry is saving us anything. I now carry a cell phone that not only makes and receives calls, but sends and receives email and keeps my calendar and contact list. It will even automatically synchronize with the computer in my office so everyone knows where the heck I'm going. I think it's my electronic security blanket, but I can't help remember it was a little simpler when this stuff wasn't around.

Today, our family, friends, co-workers and clients expect us be instantaneously available. Gone are the days when a client would call only to find out I was out of the office and not have a problem with a return call the next day. Today, they know I can be reached by cell so they expect a response right away, even if it can wait until tomorrow. I think the majority of calls made by cell phones are frivolous. I was at our local school earlier this year to pick up my son and was watching the kids as they exited the building. Most had cell phones in their hands and were dialing as soon as they hit the door. The odd thing was I think most of them were calling their friends they had walked out with or spent most of the day with. Adults are just as bad. I played in a golf tournament recently with a guy who after every hole had to call one of his buddies who was playing in the same tournament just to see how he was scoring. I wondered if they maintained the same line of communication when they got home to their respective significant others in the evening.

Electronic mail or email is just as bad. I must receive 40-60 emails a day. While there are many that do have value, I am really tired of the online drugstores, off shore casinos, low mortgage rates and, of course, the hundreds of beautiful lonely housewives that simply must meet me. The computer experts at my office work hard to filter this garbage out, but it can sneak in the system every now and again.

I am trying to revolt against the electronic age just a little. I still like to write notes and send them via the US mail. I may get a lot of calls on my cellular phone, but I let most go to voice mail and decide when to return the call later. I have always preferred to read the newspaper at home after dinner and work the crossword puzzle with a pencil. I don't have a portable DVD player to keep me company when I fly. I use the time to catch up on reading a good novel.

Every time some new technology hits the streets, I can't help but think these things that are supposed to make our lives easier are actually making them more complicated. I'd like to ponder on that a little more, but my cell phone is ringing, the emails are piling up, the fax machine is out of paper and the remote starter on my truck is acting up.

And that's the situation as I survey it…

"Jury Duty"

I had an opportunity recently to be a part of our judicial process. I was selected for jury duty. When I got the letter in the mail saying I was chosen to be a member of a pool, I had thoughts that ranged from, "I'm too busy" to "I wonder if I can still get email inside the courthouse". Of course, since I had a few weeks before the dates were coming up I watched a couple episodes of "Law and Order" on TV to brush up on what every good juror should be expected to know.

In our county, we have an opportunity to call the night before and verify if we even need to show up the next day. When I dialed the number, part of me hoped I wouldn't have to report, but another part of me was curious as to the process. I was in fact told I had to report, so I went to sleep a little apprehensive as to what I should expect. I got to the jury room bright and early and was told I could help myself to a cup of coffee. I guess this was their way of trying to make up for the $12 the county would pay me for my time that day. I found a seat and began to check email.

After a short period, the person in charge of the jury room read us a few instructions and showed us a video of what to expect. What I found interesting is the number of people that were called. The person in charge said our county had over 330,000 eligible jurors and about 28,000 were called every year. I guess I understand now why I was only getting $12 to be there. The video was very informative and after it was over we were told some of us were going to a court room to see who would be seated for a trial starting soon. I thought I might miss that draw, but nope, I was one of those chosen to head into the courtroom.

When we got there (probably 60 of us or so), we remained standing until the judge asked us to be seated. She did a great job of explaining what the case was and what we were going to do next. My stomach was churning a little. This wasn't a case of a young offender helping himself to a five finger discount in a party store. It was an *alleged,* pre-meditated first degree murder case! "Just like Law and Order", I told myself only this was very real! We were introduced to the attorneys, the defendant and we heard a list of witnesses. While I wasn't seated with the first 14 jurors in the jury box, it wasn't long before enough were excused and I heard my number called. It was my turn to be seated.

The alleged crime had occurred almost a year ago and I really didn't remember reading anything about it. I didn't know any of the people that were attached to the case, so it looked like I was going to be a fixture at the trial. That was until the judge asked me if I would be able to serve for a minimum of two weeks. I told her I was scheduled to be out of state on business toward the end of the second week. It was a trip that had been planned for several months. Before she could think about it, the prosecutor came to his feet and said he didn't believe it would take the full two weeks. The judge sat back for a second and said, "No, Mr. Prosecutor, I believe it will. Mr. Matonich, you are excused." I thanked her and quickly left the courtroom.

As I was leaving, I could see the eyes of some of my fellow jurors. It was a mixed look from "you lucky dog" to "are you sure you have a trip?" I also had mixed feelings. I really did have to travel out of state, but somehow felt I let the system down by not being there to perform my civic duty. I couldn't help but wonder about the process and what was in store for the people involved. One thing I felt very comfortable with was the process to select and train members of the jury. It was very clear and very fair. I felt certain that the fourteen members who were chosen would be a very good representation of our community and a fair trial was going to happen. I have heard once your name has been pulled, you can be assured you will be called again. Even though it does take time to go through the process, the ability to be tried by a jury of your peers is one of our greatest founding principles. I would do the best I can if called. We were told by the court that episodes of "Law and Order" were NOT good training for jurors. Maybe I could find some old episodes of Perry Mason....

And that's the situation as I survey it...

"Travel Issues"

Have you ever thought of the number of things you need to do in your life that drive you absolutely out of your mind? No matter what you do or where you live, there are things that I'm sure make you crazy, but are not in your control to realistically change. They may be little things or they may be very significant in your lives. For example, I knew a couple who fought like cats and dogs whenever they were together. Each blamed the other for saying or doing things to irritate, but when asked why they stayed together neither could see their lives apart.

For me it would be air travel. My need to board airplanes has exponentially increased over the past several years and my distaste for doing it is growing at the same pace. It never ceases to amaze me how inconsiderate some travelers can be. The airlines make it pretty clear, for example, how many carry-ons you can take aboard, but it never fails I will see one or two travelers a flight that look as though they have most of their outdated wardrobe with them stuffed in 2 or 3 oversized bags. Not only do they violate the number allowed, but these bags would barely fit in the cargo area let alone the overhead compartment on the plane. Of course it means extra time has to be spent trying to convince "Joe Passenger" his bag can't be squeezed under the seat and has to be checked. Some might say the choice is simple; don't go, but my family has grown accustomed to three meals a day and would appreciate it if I stayed gainfully employed.

Another alternative for flying is to get in the car and drive. I do enjoy driving and like the fact I can control my own destiny to a degree rather than be tied to air traffic control and the weather patterns. Unfortunately, I don't always have the extra time available to be behind the wheel. I do know a gentleman from Alaska who doesn't fly and drives to the meetings we both attend across the country. I admire his fortitude to take the extra time necessary to get from our 49th state to Washington, DC and back home again, but wonder what would happen if the meetings were ever held in Hawaii. I don't know if there is a car ferry that travels that far.

Driving isn't always an easy answer either. Big cities usually mean big traffic jams and nothing is more frustrating that sitting dead stop in the middle of 5 lanes of traffic. It is usually about that time I hear a plane take off overhead and of course would trade the traffic jam for an oversold flight full of carry-ons.

I am obviously trying to make the case for passengers to check their luggage rather than trying to carry on, but I just got back from a long flight with a number of stops and low and behold I am missing a bag. I'm not sure it could be helped, due to some very short connection times, but none the less I now have to wait for the bag to be located and brought to me just in time to re-pack it for the next flight. I may have to become one of those carry on passengers. I wonder if my golf clubs would fit under a seat as many air travelers seem to think. It couldn't hurt to try.....

And that's the situation as I survey it...

"Yellow Birch Stump"

Have you ever been in a situation that was bad enough, but once your friends and family found out about it, they managed to make it worse? I try to avoid these at all costs, but occasionally I find myself smack dab in the middle of one. This past deer season was one of those situations. I arrived at deer camp a few days before the season opener. There are several reasons for arriving early and many of them are legitimate. We really had a great time at camp this year, but had to contend with something we don't normally have to in the first few days of the season....about 30 inches of snow. The Great Lakes this past summer reached record temperatures and when Lake Superior gets warmer (even a degree or two) it means lots of snow in the west end of Michigan's Upper Peninsula. When you couple that with wet fall conditions and freezing temperatures it can create a mess. Our success rate was down due to these conditions, but camp was still a great place to be. As I usually do, I spend the first week at camp, travel back "below the bridge" to spend a few days at home and then return with my son in time for turkey day dinner and a few more days of camp life and some hunting. All this was going according to plan and I was about to leave camp after the first several days of the season. It had misted the night before I left and the snow-covered camp road turned into a sheet of ice. I knew this when I left early that morning because I almost fell off the steps coming down from the deck. I threw my gear in the back of the truck in the darkness and off I went.

I didn't travel ¾ of a mile on the camp road when I felt my truck sliding. The next thing I knew I was headed for the small ditch along side the road. "No big deal", I thought. "The ditch is full of snow and I'm not going that fast". Well, I was right.

The ditch was full of snow…just enough to cover about a 3 ½ foot tall 6" diameter yellow birch stump in the bottom of the ditch. I managed to hit the stump pretty much head on and dead center in the front of my truck. Needless to say, I wasn't a happy camper. I got out and immediately saw I wasn't going anywhere soon. The transmission cooler neatly tucked behind the bumper I had just smashed had ruptured and there was pink fluid all over the pile of snow I had so neatly pushed up. Worse than anything I had to walk back to camp to get help and figure out how I was going to make the 550 mile trip back downstate.

I walked back to camp in the darkness of the very early morning and was dreading the harassing I knew was coming my way. I thought my brother and the boys still at camp would take it easy for a while showing genuine concern, but it wouldn't be long before the gloves would come off. After the questions about my health were answered and what happened were out of the way we settled on solving the problem at hand, getting my truck out of the ditch and getting myself on the road back downstate. Using my Onstar phone we were able to get a tow truck pretty quickly. He assessed the damage and said my truck wasn't going anywhere but to his shop and I would have to rent a car to get home. He would fix the truck enough to make it road worthy and I could pick it up before Thanksgiving and get back home to have the body work done. It sounded like a great option and I was ready to go.

After he pulled the truck out of the ditch and got it set up to be towed to town, I noticed a piece of headlight trim lying on top of the snow 10 feet off the road. It must have flipped off when I lost the physics battle with the yellow birch stump. I saw my brother looking at the same piece of trim. I knew if he got his hands on it, I would regret it, but neither of us wanted to wade out in the snow to get it. I had no choice and finally went in waist deep in the snow drift and retrieved it. My brother innocently asked me why I wanted the trim piece and I told him to never mind, and put it in the back of my truck about to be towed to town. Feeling as though I had avoided a potential problem with the trim, I focused on getting to town and finding a car to drive home in.

That part of the trip went fine and just a few days later I found myself heading back north with my son to retrieve my truck and see if we couldn't finally have a successful hunt. When I went to pick up my truck and transfer our clothes and such from the rental car I noticed the piece of trim I had so gallantly fought for was missing. A cold chill went up my spine and could only hope someone from the repair shop had disposed of it and it didn't fall into the wrong hands.

When my son and I got to camp, we were greeted by my worst fears. Hanging on one of the camp walls next to the numerous sets of deer horns from many years of past successful hunts was my piece of trim. I guess it was also a trophy of some sort. I could see it was not just displayed, but it also had something written on it. I stepped closer and read: "Yellow Birch Stump 1, Johnnie Big Time 0, November 19, 2005". It was bad enough I had to go through the trauma of the accident, but now for generations to come this ordeal will live on. My brother simply smiled and thanked me for wading in the snow to get the trim and saving him the trip. A very wise man told me once "You can pick your friends, but you can't pick your relatives." How right he was.

And that's the situation as I survey it…

"Treasure Hunting"

I recently saw another anniversary of a pretty important day in history come and go. The event being the day a fine lady, Betty Matonich, gave birth to her number one son, John. As I continue to celebrate these anniversaries, I can't help but smile as I try to age gracefully, but instead fall into the mold of getting older and not so much wiser. Age really doesn't bother me, but some of the traits are a little troublesome not only to me, but to my family.

Just before Fathers' Day last year my bride asked me what I would like as a gift. I'm never too bashful about receiving a present, but this time it was difficult to think of something. I had pondered for a day or two when it hit me. I decided I needed a metal detector. I remembered running into a guy once when I was hunting who had one. He was using it in a clearing that once was the site of a logging camp. He said he had done a bunch of research on the area and could even describe how the camp was laid out. I was fascinated by his story and found myself thinking about life in a logging camp before the turn of the century. My new friend went on to tell me how he had found many sites of old logging camps and using his trusty metal detector, he had found a bunch of "treasure", from old coins to jewelry to silverware.

I guess something triggered that memory and I knew I had to have my own metal detector for Fathers' Day. I approached my wife and told her I had decided on a Fathers' Day gift. I handed her a description of the metal detector I wanted. Of course, I had spent several hours on the Internet researching to find the right one and had printed a page out of a catalog to insure I would get it. When I handed it to Ellen she kind of looked at me with a funny expression and asked if I was feeling ok. I assured her I was and wondered what the problem was. She said she had this vision of me wearing sandals with black socks and plaid shorts strolling through a park with a safari hat in search of bottle caps. She felt I wasn't old enough yet to have a metal detector. I told her I didn't even own a pair of plaid shorts and I wanted to take the detector up north to explore the old camp sites I spent years hunting around. Reluctantly, she gave in and presented me with my own detector all wrapped up in its box. It also came with a copy of a treasure hunting magazine and I delighted in relating stories to her about finding rings and coins and such to the point I thought Ellen was going to run screaming from the room.

Well, the day came when I was able to take my present up north to our cottage. I had read the instructions a dozen times and couldn't wait to take the digging tools that had come with it and go to work finding some treasure. I hadn't been searching a few seconds when the earphones erupted. I carefully dug around and lo and behold there it was…..an old fashion pull tab. Undaunted, I continued my search. Thirty minutes later, I had found three more pull tabs, a piece of wire and a rotted soup can. By this time Ellen had come out on the deck to enjoy the day and see just how bad I was doing. Of course, I explained treasure wasn't going to be found on the first try. She just shook her head and began to read her book. It wasn't too much longer when I heard a totally different sound in the earphones. My heart raced as I dug a little and finally found something of value…..a penny. I triumphantly held up my newly discovered treasure and said, "See, I knew this was worth it. If this is here there must be more." I decided to savor my loot and took a break to have a drink. I set the penny on the railing of the deck so the whole family could share in the spoils of the search. For some strange reason no one had the same feeling of victory that I had.

I have used the detector a few more times since last summer and other than a few more pull tabs I have found a grand total of three pennies; but, none were more important than the first one. What I failed to tell my family is I remembered shortly after finding it that I had thrown the penny there myself the previous Fall when I found it in the bottom of my pants pocket. Oh well, a little detail not really important compared to the thrill of discovery. I know this coming summer will bring even more opportunities to explore and go in search of whatever could be buried out there. I have had this unusual desire, though, to get a pair of plaid shorts. I guess Fathers Day isn't too far away.

And that's the situation as I survey it...

"Mickey"

I recently lost a very good friend. We met about 13 years ago and I can't tell you how much he touched my life. His love for me was unwavering. His loyalty was unquestioned. I have never had a friend like this before and I doubt I ever will again. This friend was my dog Mickey. I have had many dogs before in my life. We raised hunting dogs when I was growing up and also had the assortment of house dogs, but none of them ever touched me as much as our Mickey.

I met him on a spring day at a client's house about 3 hours north of where I live. It seemed a local, run-of-the-mill beagle found his way inside the pen of my client's field champion Brittany Spaniel who was "in season" and the next thing you know, a litter of pups arrived. My client wasn't very happy since pups from his Brittany, when properly paired, brought a good price and usually turned out to be very productive hunters, but this lot was going to be hard enough to give away. He mentioned several times during my twice-weekly visits how I surely could use a pup of my own.

Well, although I am a dog lover, I knew the lovely lady I called my wife wasn't and keeping her happy meant a lot of peace for everyone. I mentioned the new pups to her over dinner one evening in casual conversation and she gave me the "don't even think about it" look. Of course she was right. We both worked. We had enough to do to take care of our small children without adding a pup to the family. I thought about it for a while and, maybe it was my upbringing or maybe it was the fact we did have two small children, but something told me on the next trip north I was coming home with a pup.

It was a week or so before I went back to his place. I finished my business on the project and stopped by my client's to say hello. As usual he greeted me with a handshake and a smile, but this time he pulled me close and whispered, "Those pups are old enough now to leave their Ma." I didn't know what to say. I heard the voice of my wife in the background but it went away when I looked over and saw the litter playing together in the backyard. I figured I had made her mad before and was destined to do it again, so what the heck. I watched the group play for a while and hollered out to the pups, "Hey!!" Every one of those pups scattered looking for their mother – except one. This one's ear perked up and he turned toward me and ran over as fast as those pudgy little legs would allow with an odd look on his face. I knew right then and there which one was my choice. "I'll take this one." I told my client. "Have you got a box to put him in for the ride home?" He came up with something and off we went.

About half way home, I wasn't so sure I made the right decision. The new pup had thrown up twice and ate two big holes in the side of the box. I could feel the long reach of my good wife like an icy blast of cold air on my neck. As I got closer to home I called her at work and said, "Hi Babe. Do you love me?" She responded, "You are bringing home a dog, aren't you?" Oops, busted. I fessed up and after getting the lecture I deserved I could tell she was softening a little. She even volunteered to get some food, a kennel and, of course, a collar and leash.

Even though my bride never admitted to being a dog lover, she "kind of" bonded with Mickey and made sure he was treated right. She had some rules, though. There was to be no table food fed to the dog. He couldn't be anywhere near us when we were eating and there were certain rooms in the house he simply was not allowed in. He also spent his nights in a kennel and couldn't even think about getting on a piece of furniture. To my surprise he learned all those rules very quickly and rarely, if ever, broke them. Of all the dogs I raised, he was by far the most intelligent. No matter what happened to me during the day or night, I knew I would come home to at least one friendly soul. Even if it was way past the time when I should have been home, Mickey always forgave me and even knew to keep his distance the next morning when I was trying to shake off the night before.

The years finally caught up with my pal and we could all see he was slipping. We took him to his favorite Vet and were told he had developed a tumor. Our options were limited. We decided to keep him comfortable so he could spend his remaining time as happy as possible. He was never in pain, but before long just about any physical activity (including getting up from his bed) was too much for him. I knew the time had come and we let the kids know the only choice we had. My daughter came home from college and, along with my son, said their goodbyes.

My wife, being the rock she is, knew I would be a basket case taking Mickey for his last ride, so she insisted she would do it the next day. Later that night, she was working in the kitchen and I was in the family room where Mickey was laying in his bed. I could hear him breathing heavily and knew we were doing the right thing. I got up, went into the kitchen and grabbed a couple pieces of lunchmeat and a couple pieces of cheese. As I sat back down in the family room, Mickey turned over, as he had done a thousand times before, to see what I had in my hand. As I watched him I couldn't help myself and threw a piece of meat over to him. He couldn't believe it but it was gone in a flash. Next I tossed a piece of cheese, then the next piece of lunchmeat and finally the last piece of cheese. They all disappeared. He struggled to get up, and as he walked over to me, he peered into the kitchen looking at his mistress and then to me with an odd look on his face. It reminded me of the time we first met. I rubbed him behind his ears and knew I had made the right choice almost 13 years earlier. Goodbye old friend. I hope I get to rub you under your ears again someday.

And that's the situation as I survey it...

"Leaving Home"

I recently celebrated a milestone with my company. I can now say I have been with my firm over 25 years. That may not sound like much as many people have been at their jobs over 30 or 40 years. I have read about some folks who have been with the same company a lot longer than that. What makes me reflect on my tenure is how it all came to be.

When I graduated from college 25 years ago, I wasn't really sure where I would land. I knew the economy at the time was very weak and the chances of being able to stay in my native Upper Peninsula were slim and none. Actually, being able to even stay in Michigan was questionable. I lucked out. I got an offer from a Michigan firm near Flint. I didn't know much about Flint at the time. As it were, I had only traveled "below the bridge" a few times in my life, but this was a paying job and I was ready to go to work. I remember loading every single thing I owned in the back of my well-worn 1969 Buick LaSabre. I found out later that Flint was known as "Buick City" so I felt it was fate I ended up there. My cargo included some clothes, a black and white TV, a few boxes of books, a few dishes, an old webbed aluminum chaise lounge chair and some amenities for the bathroom.

I remember how upset my mother was when it was time to go. She knew I would be 550 miles away and wasn't going to be home for supper. I gave her a hug and told her I would be back to visit when I could and then left the confines of my little hometown. I found my way to the big city and started to get acclimated. I soon found an apartment (unfurnished, of course) and was given directions to one of the one-stop shopping mega stores close by to get some groceries and such.

After shopping, I pulled up to my new address and started unloading. A young lady was giving the apartment a good cleaning and asked when the movers were coming. I set the TV on the floor, plugged it in, opened up the chaise lounge chair, popped the top off a cold beer and said, "Sweetheart, this is all there is and it doesn't get any better than this."

I was able to return home a few weeks later to attend a friend's wedding and to load up on rummage sale goodies my mother had found to help fill up the almost empty apartment. She was still upset when I left, but has since gotten used to seeing my tail lights over the last 25 years as I have come and gone. I have added a wife, two kids, a house, a mortgage, and a whole bunch of stuff. I don't know how many sets of tires I would wear out if I had to use that old Buick to move today.

Being so far from where I grew up has always weighed on me. I continue to have many friends and family back home and try to see them whenever I can. They have a lot of sympathy for me when they know it's time to leave and make that nine hour drive back downstate. I used to let myself feel bad about not living where I was born, until I did some family tree research and found out I can't hold a candle to my grandfather.

What I discovered is my grandfather left Croatia and landed on Ellis Island in August of 1907. I knew he was born in 1889. Doing the math means he landed on US soil at the ripe old age of 18. Another item I know is he never returned to his native land, and my great grandparents never stepped foot in the USA. This means when he gave his mother a hug and boarded his ship in 1907, it was the last time they saw each other. They both probably knew it would be the last hug as he left, but the draw to the "New World" was too strong to keep him in

Croatia. Grandpa traveled with his cousin and once they landed, they both headed for Chicago and to other relatives who had made the journey before them. After Chicago and some stops along the way, my grandfather, his wife and a couple of kids ended up in the west end of Michigan's Upper Peninsula where my father and his future family were born.

The reality of what he and countless others did in coming to America still amazes me and gives me reason to pause and reflect on my own journey away from home. Without their fortitude, many of us wouldn't be here in the first place. I admire that kind of courage, but one thing I can do today my grandfather couldn't, is return home and give my mother another hug. She deserves it and as I think about it, a trip back home needs to be in my immediate future.

And that's the situation as I survey it…

"Busted"

Being human, it's only natural we tend to make mistakes. Sometimes they're small and sometimes they're a little larger. It's what we do with them that sets the tone for what kind of a person we really are. I have made my share of mistakes along the way, some small and some not, but have always tried to learn from them and work darn hard not repeat them.

Back when I was about 16, my mother drove a 1973, green, Ford Pinto station wagon. She really liked that car. It wasn't the least bit fancy, but it got her where she wanted to go. While it wasn't new, it was the newest car she had ever owned. I kind of enjoyed that car too. Even though I had worked hard to save money and buy my own pick-up truck, it was much older and a lot more tired than this quick little four-on-the-floor station wagon. My mother knew me all to well and rarely let me drive her car.

I asked her constantly to let me "borrow" her little wagon and take it "up town" where my friends were waiting to decide what level of mischief we were going to get into that evening. As I mentioned, she knew me all too well and refused. One evening she actually consented to me driving the Pinto. I couldn't believe it. I guess I had been extra good for awhile (which translates to not getting caught). I gave her a hug and carefully pulled away from the curb. My hands were at ten and two on the steering wheel and only one left the wheel to shift very calmly through the gears.

This lasted until I knew I was far enough out of both visual and hearing range. I stopped at a stop sign, carefully placed the gear shift in first gear and revved the engine to about redline. I then quickly let out the clutch and listened to those little 13 inch tires squeal down the street. Imagine my glee when I hit second gear and it squealed the tires again. I could see this was going to be a great night.

After picking up a few of my friends and stopping at the local drive-in for root beers and hot dogs, we set off to find the perfect stretch of asphalt to work on the "laying of the patch" as us race car drivers referred to it. We found such a freshly paved street and proceeded to have a great time. With the AM music blasting on the radio and half empty root beer containers in hand we went to work on the "perfect patch". All was right with the world until I got a little over zealous in attempting to back up to the homemade starting line. As I pushed the gear shift over and up to find reverse, imagine my horror when the gear shift pulled right out of the transmission housing in my hand.

It took about 2 seconds for my buddies to figure out what happened and like rats fleeing a sinking ship they vanished into the night. After a few choice "Oh darns", I had to think how I could learn from this mistake and more importantly escape without serious bodily injury from my mother. I was able to get the shift lever back in the housing, but a piece of the metal ears that did the shifting was definitely broken off and glue wasn't going to work on this one. "Think, think," I said to myself and then it came to me. I had a good friend who worked at a gas station about 4 miles away. Now this wasn't any gas station. It was a "full service" gas station. You must remember the kind. They pumped your gas, washed your windows, and checked your oil. All with a smile and you didn't have to slip your credit card in a tray under 1" thick plexi-glass. More importantly, this station also did repair work and had a welder in the garage. Just the thing that could help rectify this mistake.

As I thought, my buddy was working that night and between the two of us, we were dangerous enough with a welder to fix the broken shifter and get it back into place as good as new. In fact, I was pretty proud of that little welding job and patted myself on the back as I headed for home. I turned the corner slowly and coasted down the street and eased the Pinto Wagon back where it was only hours before safe and sound. I shut the door as it should have been and went in the house and up to bed.

The next day I heard my mother start up her car and drive away. I could hear the sound of her shifting and it never missed a beat. I fell back into a relaxed sleep. Later that evening, after finishing our supper, my mother calmly looked over at me and said, "Of course, you will never drive my car, again." I was horrified. How did she find out? Did the weld not hold? I was about to start explaining about the shifter when I stopped myself from making yet another terrible mistake. I simply looked up at her and asked, "Why?" It turns out when I originally left the house the night before and thought I was out of hearing range, I wasn't. My mother heard the first squeal of the tires and I was busted. But, the mistake I didn't make was to open my mouth and make the whole thing worse. I hope she doesn't read this column. I never did drive her car again, but I also never told her the rest of the story either. Even today, I think that might be a mistake.

And that's the situation as I survey it…

"Poncho's Heater"

I was with a group of my buddies not too long ago and it usually doesn't take much time before the conversation turns to some of the not so brilliant things we may have done in our youth. I really enjoy those stories and even contribute a few of my own every now and again. Sometimes, they involve other friends or perhaps a member of our own families.

My father has been gone about 11 years now. He wasn't the easiest guy to grow up with and at times was pretty hard on us kids. He was a consummate laborer and if it had to be dug up or moved, piled or unpiled, he was the right guy for the job. He left most complicated thinking to others, and of course, wasn't then subjected to any blame if the plan went awry. Every now and then though, he would out-fox himself and we would get to smile about it.

More than 15 years ago, my younger brother, Pete, bought an existing deer camp in an area he enjoyed hunting. It wasn't much of a camp, but it was a start. He has since built a new one and it is by far one of the finest deer camps on or near the Mosinee Grade. Along with this camp came the need to get some deer blinds ready for the season. One of the luxuries you can have in these blinds is a little portable propane heater. They do a great job of taking the chill out of the blind which means it is easier to hunt much longer. When I hunted with Dad as a young lad, we didn't have anything at all like this set up.

We hunted from home which meant getting up even earlier to be out in the woods before dawn and getting home a lot later after dark. There were no blinds to sit in, let alone heaters to keep you warm. We sat out all day on tree stumps or piles of pine boughs, so the concept of a camp and deer blinds was kind of foreign to my father. On top of that he was a proud man and saw any movement toward luxuries as a sign of weakness. He quickly bought into the idea of hunting from camp, though, as he could rationalize less drive time and gas wasted. The idea of hunting out of a blind was a little tougher, but he came to realize he wasn't getting any younger and not being totally exposed to the elements wasn't a terrible idea. He drew the line at the idea of a heater. It was like the last straw for him. My brother told him he would get him a propane heater as a present, but that even made Dad more determined. You see, getting presents was also a sign of weakness. I told you it wasn't easy growing up around him.

One sunny day in mid-fall with deer season only a few short weeks away, my brother stopped by the family house and found our father in the backyard sitting at the picnic table working on some god-ugly contraption. It seems the more Dad thought about the heater thing, the more he understood it may be nice to be warm during the day, but would be damned if he would go out and buy a new unit. It seems he found an abandoned collapsed camp in his travels while bird hunting that fall. While rooting around in the remains, he came across this antiquated little heater that ran on fuel oil. It was a very early attempt at portable heat and while my brother wasn't sure how well this was going to work, Dad had it cleaned up and running right there on the picnic table. My brother said it was throwing off heat and was actually humming along quite well. Pete just shook his head, wished Dad well and left.

Soon enough, it was opening day of deer season. My father headed out to his blind early in the morning and my brother to his. It wasn't very long before the sun came up and soon after my brother was able to bag his buck. After preparing it for the trip, he started his way back to camp. He had to pass quite close to my father's blind so he thought he would swing by and show Dad his deer (as well as checking on him, too). As he got closer to the blind, he could see something was horribly wrong. There was black smoke billowing out of every crack and opening that existed in the blind. He stepped up the pace now and just as he reached the blind, the little side door opened up and my father's "free" fuel oil heater came flying out of the doorway tumbling across the landscape into a nearby snow pile. My father followed closely after the heater. My brother said when he saw Dad come out of the blind he almost burst out laughing. Dad was covered from head to toe in thick, black soot. Pete said until Dad blinked he couldn't see his eyes. Dad was doing his best to start a line of cuss words that would have embarrassed anyone, but each time he started to speak all that came out was a little puff of black smoke. That was too much to take and Pete couldn't help but start to laugh.

He took Dad back to camp and got him cleaned up. Dad didn't think the whole thing was all that funny until later, but he did get all the soot out of his system and was able to finally properly swear at the blankety blank heater. It seems it wasn't running correctly right from the time Dad lit it. The more he tried to adjust it in the dark, the more soot it threw off until he finally kicked it out of the blind.

I have heard this story several times and can't help but laugh when I picture my Dad covered in soot and not being able to swear. I guess a day or so later Pete came back to camp and found Dad fiddling with yet another heater. This one was much newer than the first and did run on propane but was nowhere near brand new. Pete didn't want to ask where it came from and Dad wasn't offering. He just looked up at Pete and said, "A little cleaning and adjusting and I will have this thing working like one of your fancy store bought ones." Pete just shook his head, reached in a cabinet and took out an extra roll of paper towel.

And that's the situation as I survey it...

"Good Old Days"

As we move into a new year and all get just a little older, I like to think back on times when things were much different. Presently, there is almost no point in a day when you can't conduct some kind of business. You can shop 24/7 for about anything you would like in the mega-marts that may only be closed one or two days a year. On those unique occasions when they might be closed or you are too tired to travel, you can turn to your trusty computer and order it "online". With the sophisticated tracking sites you can even watch the progress of your merchandise as it makes its way across town, the state or even the country. I feel kind of sorry for the delivery drivers as they must feel as though the world is watching them for the entire time they are on the job.

When I was a lot younger and living in my small hometown, it was much different. Stores weren't open at all hours and business had to be conducted in person or via snail mail. You could call the local J.C. Penney or Sears store and place a catalog order, but you didn't very often get a good prediction as to when you might see your merchandise. Also in those days most of the gas stations were called "Service Stations" because they not only pumped gas, but could service any other needs of your car. But they didn't sell milk or bread or tacos or fried chicken. If you needed milk at 7 pm during the week or anytime on Sunday, you better have a good neighbor. I can recall once on a Sunday when I was about 12 years old, I needed a 9 volt battery and was absolutely shut out as no stores were open and the service stations that were open (as not all were on a Sunday) only carried car batteries. They were a little too big to fit inside my transistor radio.

Going to the bank was also an experience. Monday through Thursday the bank was open to transact business only until the appointed time of 3:30 pm. After that time the doors were locked so all the books could be balanced and the staff could be home by 5 pm to have supper with their families and then go to the local high school to watch a basketball game. There were no ATMs, no drive-up windows or even on-line banking, yet everyone seemed to get their business done. Fridays were the one day that the rules changed. Stores stayed open until 8:30 pm. The bank stayed open until 7:30 pm. It was the one time of the week when the town was completely buzzing with activity. Paychecks got cashed. Groceries were purchased. Friends chatted on the street. Weekend project hardware found its way into the back of a station wagon and you may have even found time to have a root beer float at the local soda fountain. It seemed everyone knew it was the time to get their shopping done so other things in life could happen later.

I sometimes miss those days, but can't argue with the convenience of today's world. I don't have to worry if I need a 9 volt battery or a loaf of bread or gallon of milk. Only a short drive away is one of many open stores to help me out of a jam (or with jam, if I need it). I also have to admit the online shopping can be pretty convenient as well. Thirty minutes or so with a credit card and you can buy just about anything for anybody. You don't have to fight traffic or bad roads or the weather. But the one thing today's lifestyle doesn't do is find the time for friends to simply run into each other on the street and chat. Catching up on what's been happening today seems to be done through things like "MySpace.com" or Instant Messaging. I do also miss the root beer floats at the Tip-Top restaurant on a Friday night in downtown Bessemer and I don't think they would taste the same if I ordered them from Sodafountain.com.

And that's the situation as I survey it...

"Like Father Like Son"

Hello, my name is John and I'm a gadget boy. I can't help it, but I admit I am hooked on gadgets. I like things that do things I typically never need but have to have anyway. My truck has heated, 75 way power seats that I set when I first got the truck and haven't touched since. I have never had the heating feature on. The radio has 6 screens each holding 6 stations, yet I always listen to the same one. The truck also has a blue button that once pushed supposedly allows you to get directions, make reservations and check the weather anywhere in the world. Well, I rarely get lost, usually don't need reservations to eat and can tell the weather by looking out the window. But I had to sign up for the service, just in case.

My family knows I have this terrible affliction, but sometimes tends to add to it. I got an iPod for Christmas this year (OK, I did have it on my wish list) and within four hours had loaded several movies and a couple of audio books. I ordered a cable to run the gadget into my truck's stereo system (keeping in mind I only listen to one radio station) and connector cords that are retractable. The normal ones were too bulky, I told myself. I got a real cool case to put it in, along with a car charger, wall charger, TV adaptor, ear buds, instruction manual and a couple of wires I have no clue what they are for. I don't have any music on it, but will be able to charge it anywhere, anytime once it needs it.

A few years ago I bought a handheld GPS unit so I wouldn't get lost in the woods where I hunt. I am only a mile or so off the main road (traffic sounds are quite easily heard) and am bounded by a river and another road on the remaining three sides, I justified this acquisition by telling myself you never know where you may end up. I still carry two compasses (one of which is a gadget unto itself) and use the GPS unit to get the altitude of my deer blind and barometric pressure. I am not sure why I need either of those facts, but I will be ready if I figure it out. I can tell you it is 399.4 miles (as the crow flies) from my easy chair at home to the chair in my deer blind. This information was pretty useful until last year when we moved my blind 40 or 50 yards so I had to punch in new coordinates. It is now 399.3 miles.

My bride just shakes her head and gives me the "look" whenever this affliction raises its ugly head. She knows there is little hope for my cure and has simply learned to ignore it. Although it was she that dubbed me the "gadget boy", she now has someone else to shake her head over. It seems my son has developed much of the same disease. He has a couple of guitars, multiple amps and a ton of cables. I have to admit he does like to play them, but every time he mentions some new addition to his collection, his mother gives me the "look" that says he has inherited my genetic deficiency. To make matters worse, he plans to attend my Alma Mater next fall and surely will be exposed to more gadgets in their engineering department than he ever imagined before.

Even now, if you need something technical to work or to be put together he is the guy to do it. I watch him on the computer typing what seems faster than the speed of light while I continue to use the hunt and peck method. His cell phone has about every bell and whistle available and he has figured out most of them He usually has the latest video game mastered quickly and stays on top of what the next version will be. I guess he is his father's son and I shouldn't be surprised. I knew it years ago when I gave him his own handheld GPS unit and the first thing he figured out was that it was 399.4 miles from our family room to my deer blind.

And that's the situation as I survey it...

"Early Riser"

I was discussing my kids sleep habits with some friends the other day. I wasn't really complaining, but I was expressing how odd I thought these habits were. It seems being up late at night and sleeping as long as possible the next day is quite a common practice. My son and I had just returned from a trip to our place in Michigan's "God's Country" and I think he spent more time on his back than on his feet. Now, we didn't have many chores to do and it was the time of the year when there isn't enough snow to ride the snowmobile, but too much snow to go four-wheeling so we did do a lot of nothing. I didn't mind that as I wanted a chance to just spend some bonding time. I could have bonded more if I would have sat over his bed (or the couch) and spoke to him over his snoring. I guess he was recharging his batteries and sleep was a major part of that process. As I was relating this story to friends, I stopped in mid-comment and realized I was starting to sound just like my Dad did when I was my son and daughter's age. I thought it was a little scary.

As I sat there, my mind raced back to those days living at home and I smiled as I remembered my life at that age. My father was a very early riser. I mean extremely early. He usually had downed a pot of coffee and caught the news on the local AM radio station before the sun even thought about rising. That was fine with me, but what caused the problems was he thought everyone else should be up at that time as well to share in the glory of the morning. I was never too enthused about joining him that early because I knew as soon as the sun rose there would be a list of things to do. No matter what time I got home (the older I got, the later it was) he would show up at the door to my bedroom and pace back and forth for at least

5 minutes. If the sound of his footsteps didn't wake me up, he would start coughing and clearing his throat. That usually did the trick, but of course, I ignored him in hopes he would go searching for a new pot of coffee or some latest local high school sports score. Rarely did ignoring him work and I could just feel the heat from the slow burn he was doing in the hallway. Pretty soon he couldn't help himself and he would poke his head in the door and say loudly, "Are you going to sleep the whole GD day away? We have work to do".

Of course we really didn't have anything that HAD to be done at that time of the morning, but he wanted to make sure rocks got picked out of the garden or snow got shoveled off the roof or the postage sized yard we had got mowed. Starting the mower at the crack of dawn may have got the job done, but didn't do anything for my relationship with the neighbors. Even though they knew my father was an early riser, they continued to blame me for not finding a way to seize up the mower motor so it wouldn't be heard until a more civilized time of day. I knew stalling Dad was a lost cause so I would get up, choke down a cup of now 2 hour old coffee and rehash the local news with him and try not to fall asleep at the table.

After I could see some light outside, I would take my list of to-dos, walk outside and try to find one that caused the least amount of disruption to the rest of town and get at it. After completing the items on the list, I would head back in the house fully awake, knowing I was now up for the duration. It never failed that as soon as I walked in the house I could hear snoring coming from the family room where Dad was peacefully napping on his favorite couch. Of course I wanted to pour Draino in his half drunk, 10th cup of coffee, but never did. I would simply go about my business for the rest of the day. You see I failed to mention this was Dad's modus operandi. He usually went to bed about 8 pm, got up about 4 am, took a nap at 8 am, left the house until about noon and after a bowl of soup would hit the couch again at about 1:30 pm.. I know it doesn't sound very exciting, but he was happy, so other than wanting to drag me into his world, who was I to complain?

After remembering those times, I told myself I would go a little easier on my son from now on. I guess if he wants to sleep until noon every day of a school break, I won't stand in his way. Besides I don't want him eyeballing my half-drunk cup of coffee while I am snoozing on the couch at 8 in the morning.

And that's the situation as I survey it...

"Graduation Day"

We had a big event at the Matonich household earlier this summer. Our son Matt graduated from high school. He will now join his sister in the ranks of college students and my bank account will take an additional tuition hit. I was proud of my son as I watched him walk into the auditorium wearing his cap and gown. He has grown into quite the young man and even though we scrap occasionally, he knows I love him dearly and only want the best for him. I even have a softer spot in my heart for him as this fall he will be trekking off to my alma mater, Michigan Tech. This will not only be a big step for him, but will be hard on his parents as well. Going away to College is difficult enough and being more than 500 miles away makes it even tougher. His mother will be hit the hardest as Matt has been her buddy for a long time and I know she won't like him gone, but she understands he needs to do this to help secure his own future.

As I sat through the graduation ceremony, my mind wandered back to many years earlier and my own high school graduation. It wasn't in an auditorium and didn't have 400 students receiving diplomas. It was in our school gymnasium and had 85 grads walking up to get their sheepskin. There weren't 25 open houses to go to throughout the summer either. Everyone had their open house right after graduation so you made the rounds once and you were done. I think the snow was actually gone so most were held outside. Many of the grads eventually got together later in the evening and we had a little party....well, ok we had a big party. There weren't any project graduation lock-ins back then and I am glad there are now.

I told Matt he is about to enter into a new chapter in his life and one that could help him accomplish any or all of his future goals. He looked at me with a blank stare and I realized he really didn't have any future goals at this point. I then remembered I didn't either when I was his age. I was more interested in anything but thinking of future responsibilities and I guess he is too. It will all come soon enough as it did for me. It wasn't long before I had a car full of stuff and was heading off to college, not sure what to expect, but anxious to get it going. I think Matt will be in the same boat. I am sure by the end of the summer he will be ready to spread his wings and make his mark on the world.

It is kind of ironic that he graduated from high school in 2007. I did in 1977 and my mother in 1947. All 30 years apart and how the world has changed over that time period. When my mother graduated there wasn't much talk about colleges, far more about which mine to work at and the fact the war was about over. When I graduated, college was a much stronger option. The Vietnam War and the draft were over. The mines were closed and jobs were scarce and many of my classmates had to leave the area to find work. My son's graduating class has the greatest college influence, jobs still seem to be scarce and we find ourselves plunged into a war once again.

The one constant between three generations of Matonichs is a desire to tackle the future and give it our best shot. I have seen this characteristic in Matt and know when he puts his mind to it, he can do about anything. I am proud of him for that and look forward to the day when I see him again walking down the aisle in a cap and gown. This time the choices won't be schools, but jobs and which areas to live. I guess his life decisions are just beginning and will be more challenging as time goes on. I am sure he will understand that some day soon. Who knows, we may see a fourth generation Matonich walking into an auditorium in 2037.

And that's the situation as I survey it…

"Black Bart"

As I get older, I find myself getting more and more like my father. That can be scary considering some things and good considering others. One of the things my Dad used to do while I was growing up was point out local history while we were going anywhere. It might have been as simple as who once lived at a particular home or as elaborate as the story of Black Bart. Yep, we really did have a Black Bart in the western end of Michigan's Upper Peninsula. His real name was Reimund Holzey and his story is tied to a road still known today as Stage Coach Road. It seems this road has a claim to fame. As the story goes, it is the scene of the last stage coach robbery in the nation. I find it hard to believe that anywhere east of the Mississippi could ever hold that claim, but I guess it has to be somewhere. It happened in 1889 near a resort at the south end of Lake Gogebic not far from where I grew up. It seems some businessmen from Chicago where on their way to visit their families who were spending the summer at the resort. They had taken the train to the last railroad station not far from the lake and boarded a stage coach for the last several miles of their journey. They hadn't gone far when the 22 year old woodsman jumped in front of the stage and demanded their possessions. Two men were killed in the skirmish and the young Reimund fled the scene. A posse was formed and it wasn't long before he was apprehended. According to the story, it took the jury all of 45 minutes to convict Mr. Holzey and he was sentenced to life in the Marquette prison. Mr. Holzey reportedly served 24 years before he was released in 1913. Newspaper accounts said he had "recovered from his criminal tendencies" following surgery to remove a bone splinter that had penetrated his brain.

My father and I had traveled this same road many times as I was growing up, either on our way to the lake for an evening of fishing or on a bright fall day while we were hunting partridge. It never failed that each time we passed that way, my Dad would recount the story. It didn't hold much interest for me then, but as the years passed I have grown to appreciate the history lessons more and more. It reminded me of the families in early times who relied on their elders to pass down their own family history through stories. Long before family trees and genealogy, these stories were handed down from generation to generation keeping family history alive. My Dad told me a lot of things during those trips. I have remembered quite a bit of it, not because I wanted to at the time, but because he repeated it so many times it is hard not to. Now that he is gone, I am truly grateful he did it. The stories are wonderful reminders of times past and the rich history of the area I grew up in.

My own children are now suffering the same fate as their father once did. I find myself repeating to them the stories I've heard whenever we travel the same routes. We don't live in the area, but I now have a cottage on the lake, and we try to spend as much time there as we can. I make them turn off their ipods and listen to the stories I heard as a child. I think they receive them about the same as I did, but just as my father, I don't plan to stop repeating them. I want them to always be tied to this area no matter where they end up living after college, and these stories are one way to do that.

My only regret is my father isn't around to be the story teller. I didn't appreciate it then, but he had a magical way of telling a story that I know his grandchildren would truly appreciate. In fact, they might listen better if the stories were coming from him than from their own father (imagine that). I hope someday to have the opportunity to travel down the Stage Coach Road with my own grandchildren and have them imagine the horse drawn coach, stopped as the young woodsman did his best to make history for the area. I know I will repeat myself many times, but I think that is what an elder is supposed to do.

And that's the situation as I survey it...

"Free Lunch"

One of the benefits of getting older is watching your children grow up. I am truly enjoying the fact that my kids are now growing into young adults. They are really making their own marks on the world and although I will never stop worrying about them, they seem to be doing just fine. They both are in college now and gone are the days of lunchboxes and finger paintings. Today it is debit cards and text messages. They have their own circle of friends and certainly new challenges.

Even though Matt is 550 miles from home and can't just drop in for a weekend he seems to be adjusting quite well. He has been cliff diving (don't tell his mother), gone to many social and sporting events, pledging a fraternity and claims he even finds time to study. I can only hope the latter happens more often than the former. I can tell from our communications he is coming into his own. He has chosen a tough career path at a tough university but if it works out, he will benefit from it quite well.

Katie took to college like a duck to water. She is in her last year and besides singing in the choir, belonging to a sorority, interning in our state's governor's office, she is also engaged and planning a wedding. I don't know where she gets all her energy, but she is extremely focused and quite driven. She does get to come home occasionally and is a whirlwind while she is there, but usually finds some time to sit down and fill her dad in on what's happening in her hectic life.

Katie and Matt interact with each other all the time which really makes me smile. Matt was ill a little bit ago while at college and had to go to the hospital. It was one of those calls no parent wants to get, but it all turned out fine. The next day I sent a message to Katie to let her know about her brother and she calmly informed me she already knew about it from Matt's posting on "Facebook". I am not sure what that is, but I guess it gets the word out to all who should know. I can't imagine my mother sending me a text message.

Even though the kids aren't really kids anymore, occasionally they do fall back to the old ways. I traveled up to my cottage recently and went to the "Root Cellar" to enjoy an adult beverage. It is a very nice restaurant/watering hole on my lake and is within walking distance from my place. I have gotten to know the owners Rick and Jane quite well and they are great people. After I said a few hellos to some of the folks there and sat down, Jane came over and said she needed to talk to me. It seemed my son was at the cottage with a buddy a weekend or two earlier and had dinner at the "Root" a couple of nights. She told me they were perfect gentlemen and everyone enjoyed their company. She did say though that on Saturday night Matt asked that since he paid for his supper on Friday night, could his dad pay for it on Saturday night. Jane smiled as she handed me their Saturday dinner tab and I reached for my wallet. She commented that Matt was a good tipper and judging from the fact it was coming out of my pocket, it didn't surprise me. I thanked Jane for allowing me to run the tab and smiled as I could picture my son putting that scheme together. It is funny though, he failed to mention that little episode to me. I didn't see it in any text messages either. Maybe I should have checked his "Facebook".

And that's the situation as I survey it…

"Improvements"

Anyone who knows me or who has read these ramblings over the last number of years knows how much I enjoy traveling back to the land where I was born and raised. They would also know that one of my favorite times of the year to travel home is in November for the 15 day ritual known as whitetail deer season. I am very fortunate to have a brother with a camp that I can hunt out of and many good friends to enjoy the time with, but lately I have been questioning the extremes we seemed to have gone to there. My brother's place is quite a ways from any real civilization and the only conveniences are the ones we provide for ourselves. This, however, hasn't seemed to stop the group from continually making little improvements each year to make the place even more livable and comfortable. I don't mean things like heat, lights or an inside toilet. Those were taken care of years ago with a propane heater and a generator. I thought we were living pretty high on the hog with just those additions, but they don't hold a candle to some of the changes made over the last few years.

We dug a well a while back and put in a hand pump so we wouldn't have to haul water to flush the toilet and do the dishes. We built a sauna building so we could clean up after a hard day's hunt and not offend each other after several days of not being within 2 miles of a bar of soap. We built a separate building for the generator to keep the noise to a minimum so we could play cards in peace. We added a car radio/CD player so we could listen to tunes powered by a deep cycle battery and not have to run the "jenny" all the time. We wired speakers to the outside of the camp so in the Fall when the weather is nice and the bugs are gone, we could sit outside with a cool adult beverage and listen to the ball game or some good oldies. All of these changes have made life much better at camp, but I am not sure we aren't going a little overboard.

Earlier this Fall, my brother called and asked if I had an extra color TV he could have for camp. I did have a medium sized extra set at my cottage and told him to take that, but was puzzled why, considering we didn't get many stations with our antenna and never felt the need for color. I soon found out. When I pulled into camp on a beautiful day this Fall, I was surprised to hear the generator running. We typically run it only at night and rely on batteries and gas lights during the day. Imagine my surprise when I walked in to find not just one, but two color TVs going and a bunch of buddies watching the NASCAR race. Someone else was pumping dollars into a video slot machine against the wall and in the corner of the room was a new water bubbler. I couldn't believe my eyes and had to fire down a shot of Wild Turkey to calm down (actually, I was pretty calm...I just wanted to have a shot of Turkey).

My buddies explained they were able to wire in a satellite dish at camp this year and were using a local account to acquire a receiver. It seems the water bubbler was an extra one given to us by a supplier and I noticed several large bottles of water in a corner of the camp, so I guess we were set for the season. On the deck of the camp was a new gas grill. It was further explained that the old charcoal grill was hard to regulate and it would be easier to cook steaks on the gas one.

I took all this news and all the new improvements in stride. We do spend a lot of time at camp and I do like my steaks cooked evenly. The picture on the color TV was pretty nice and I suppose watching NFL football without the normal snowy picture was going to be ok. The water coming out of the hand pump isn't terrible to drink, but the bottled water was much better. I kind of shook my head and thought of how far this whole thing had come while I was standing in line for my turn at the video slot machine. I guess I will get used to the new improvements and they will certainly make life easier on the Mosinee Grade.

I was just settling down on the stool at the slot machine, content in acceptance of all the new stuff when I thought of my father. While I have missed him terribly since he passed away a number of years ago, I was very glad he wasn't around to witness what had happened at camp. He never would have put up with all this stuff and would have made our lives miserable for even considering the upgrades. But he wasn't there so I slipped out of my boots, put on some camp slippers and settled in for a very comfortable visit....that is, until I was informed of the plans for next year. I was told we have acquired a wooden hot tub from a chalet at one of the local ski hills and a new submersible wood stove was just being completed. A pad of sand was set off one corner of the deck and it had been agreed by all involved that by next deer season we would be able to sit outside in this wood heated wooden hot tub sipping an adult beverage and listening to music on the outdoor speakers while the snow came down around us.

The last straw was when my brother pulled a battery operated Coleman blender out from under the bar and asked what flavor of Margaritas I liked. I couldn't answer him. All I could think about was my Dad coming back from the grave, bursting through the door at that very moment with a match and burning the whole place down to teach us a lesson. I waited for a minute and he didn't show up. I gave a sigh of relief and answered my brother. Ok, so maybe it is over the top, but I am not getting any younger and those comforts are pretty nice. Besides, I enjoy a margarita every now and then and having one in a hot tub at camp is as good a place as any to enjoy it. I just hope Dad never finds out.

And that's the situation as I survey it...

"Road Rules"

I know I am getting older and my basket of patience is probably more like a small cup these days, but I truly think drivers are getting worse every time I head down the road. I log quite a few miles each year, drive in all types of weather conditions and on all kinds of roadways. Rural to urban, interstate to gravel, I am on them all. Lately, it doesn't seem to matter where I am driving, I have experienced some of the most frustrating times behind the wheel. So, in order to attempt to help some of those less conscientious drivers, I have created "John's Rules of the Road". I would highly suggest if you see yourself in any of these situations, you clip this out and tape it to the visor of your car, truck, SUV, motorhome or whatever you drive, to help remind you that others are also trying to use the road with you.

Rule#1) When you are going to turn, your turn signal should be engaged **prior** to you hitting the brake pedal. It is far more helpful to those behind you to telegraph your intentions a little earlier than half way through the turn.

Rule#2) If you are going to pull out in front of me, please use the little pedal by your right foot known as the accelerator to get up to speed a little sooner than the next millennium. Nothing is more aggravating than to have someone pull out in front of me and proceed to run at half of the posted speed limit. I guess they were in a hurry to see if my brakes worked, but not in enough of a hurry to get where they are going anytime that day. The drivers that are worse are the ones who pull out in front of you (even though there are no cars behind you) only to turn right at the very next intersection. Of course, they fail to signal as well.

Rule#3) Whenever you can....**use your cruise control.** It is extremely frustrating to pass someone on the freeway only to have them pass you 5 minutes later and you them 5 minutes from then and so on. Not only does it waste fuel, it is unnerving to continually play leap frog down the road. Many times as I pass or get passed, the non cruise party looks at me puzzled as to why they are seeing me again. I have a sign made up that I simply hold up in the window that says, "Unless, you work for OPEC and don't mind $3.50 for a gallon of gas, please use your cruise control." The message usually gets through and off they go never to be seen again.

Rule#4) As long as we are talking about freeways, if you are in the passing lane....**travel at the speed necessary to pass or move back over in your original lane**. It is maddening to watch someone pull out in front of a long line of traffic only to be going 2 mph faster than the snail they are trying to pass. After what seems to be an eternity, they may actually be past the vehicle they wished to pass and pull back over, but more likely they decide to overtake the next vehicle and stay right where they are. In the mean time, several hundred vehicles and covered wagons with teams of oxen have lined up behind them waiting for the next ice age or passing completion, which ever comes first.

Rule#5) The passing lane on the freeway is not a travel lane. Unless you are an emergency vehicle the law says you are to **keep right except to pass.** It is very frustrating to come up behind a vehicle in the left lane on the freeway and have them refuse to pull over to the right even though the right lane is clear of traffic. Of course, they aren't using their cruise and aren't traveling even close to the speed limit, but they feel this lane has their name on it and they will be danged if they are going to move over. That means everyone is passing them on the right which is very unsafe and in many places illegal, but the left lane hogger could care less.

Rule#6) When you are driving....**DRIVE!** Leave the cell phone off or get hands free. Keep the make-up in your purse and wait until you get to work or get up **5 minutes earlier** and put it on at home. If you are hungry, stop and eat. I actually saw someone trying to drive the other day with a cell phone in one hand and a burger in the other. They were actually steering with their knee. This is just the person I don't want anywhere near me when I am driving especially if I have precious cargo such as children or loved ones with me.

I am sure there are many more rules to be conscious of when you are on the road, but these are just a few that, if followed, would make a whole lot more people happier and safer. I promise I will try to follow them as well, so I guess I better get my blinker fixed, learn how to work the cruise control and resolve to keep my hands on the wheel instead of my cell, although I might be able to learn that steering with the knee trick.

And that's the situation as I survey it...

"Endorsements"

It is bad enough that we have had to endure so far over 18 months of election campaign rhetoric with no end in sight, but I read an article the other day that was the last straw. I happened to be scanning the newspaper when I came across a piece reporting that the rock star, Bruce Springsteen, had given his endorsement to one of the Democratic candidates running for President. Now, it doesn't at all surprise me that Mr. Springsteen supports a candidate for President of this great country. He has always been a great American and a great musician, but what does surprise me is that his choice would be in any way shape or form, newsworthy.

I didn't realize that "The Boss" (as he is known in the music industry) spent countless hours analyzing individual candidate platforms and economic recovery plans. I must have missed his dissertation on the American impact in a global economy. Maybe I missed it because I don't believe he wrote one. So the question of the day is...why should I give a rat's patootie who Mr. Springsteen supports for President? More importantly, what journalistic bozo would even think that I do care enough to be paid to waste ink on that story. While I have the utmost respect for The Boss's musical talents, I am confused as to why the American public would care about his political leanings.

This appears to me to be a serious problem for our country. We seem to be looking to others for the answers instead of taking the time to use our own noggins to figure things out. In our quest for fast food, instant coffee and drive through banking we have also in many cases delegated our thought process to others rather than taking the time to draw our own conclusions. I am also concerned that we have fallen into the trap that makes us believe simply because an individual is good (or great) at something, they must be a genius at everything.

The list of celebrity endorsements of political candidates is a long one and continues to grow. It appears that the minute one of the candidates from either party is seen on a stage raising his or her arm with the celebrity de jour, the others aren't far behind with yet another star of stage, screen or television. I may be wrong, but did anyone else see Box Car Willie wearing one of the candidate's buttons on his latest infomercial? I am not sure what it says about this country's electorate if we are more interested in who Oprah is supporting rather than what the candidate is saying about rising fuel costs. I am also a little concerned that some of these folks are full enough of themselves that they would think their endorsement actually holds any power for their chosen candidate.

This whole situation may simply be my own lack of understanding. I don't buy cereal because it has a ball player's picture on it. I don't use the same woodworking equipment as Norm Abrams and my golf clubs are not the same ones as those used by Tiger Woods (which many of my friends say explains my golf game). The reality is I would be more inclined to listen to someone closely related to a situation than one who is not.

I would like to know who Alan Greenspan thinks is the right choice to be the leader of the greatest nation in the world. I might also be interested in who the head of economics at Harvard feels would be our best next leader. I don't suspect I will see that person in the news wearing anyone's campaign button. How about asking the head of the American Medical

Association who his choice would be to help us deal with the health care crisis in the US?

Maybe that would require actual thought process on our parts rather than simply following some media darling's lead. We may actually have to truly understand the issues instead of letting a glossy piece of mail showing a movie star's arm around one of the candidates to help make our choice. I don't know, though, I keep waiting for Zamphere to put down his pan flute on his latest infomercial and enlighten me as to who I should vote for...

And that the situation as I survey it...

"Katie Girl"

I would like to tell you a story about a little girl. She is quite special in my book and has done some extraordinary things in a relatively short period of time. When she was young it seemed she learned how to walk before she ever learned how to crawl and has never stopped moving. She drove absolutely insane at times as a baby because she never wanted to go to sleep, but the minute she looked up at me with those big brown eyes and said, "Da Da" my frustrations melted away. I don't think that has changed ever since. If you can't already tell, I am writing about my daughter, Katie.

She never ceases to amaze me with the things she can do and how strong she is in her convictions. She did catch me by surprise a few years ago when she came home from her summer job and told me she thought someone she had just met was going to ask her out on a date. I immediately went to my gun cabinet and started oiling one of my really big shotguns. She told me to put the gun back because he seemed really nice. I began to explain there aren't any really nice guys (except for Dad), but I could see her mind was made up and could tell by the look in her eye my little girl was growing up.

Well, one date lead to another and then another. I have to admit when I met him, I thought he was a nice guy too, but it didn't stop me from leaning on my gun cabinet when I was talking to him for the first time....just in case, ya know. He had a soft smile and a genuine sparkle in his eye when he and Katie were together and I knew they were happy. As a parent, it is an odd feeling to see someone come into your family that has never been there before, but it wasn't long before he fit right in. Kurt likes to play video games so he and my son, Matt, get along great. He works in the computer side of the world so I know who to call when I needed something figured out on my home computer. "Hmmmm", I said to myself, he is kind of handy to have around.

Then it happened. I was out of town on business quite a while ago and as I was flipping channels in my hotel room late one night, my cell phone rang. Since it never rings that late I hoped nothing was wrong and jumped up to answer it. I didn't recognize the number and almost let the call go to voicemail, but something told me to answer it. It was Kurt and he said he really needed to talk to me. He said he loved my daughter and he wanted to know if it was ok with me if he asked Katie to marry him. I didn't know what to say. I kind of wished I had let it go to voicemail, but I could see Katie's brown eyes in my mind and knew this was meant to be. I told Kurt absolutely not and hung up....kidding....I told him that if it was ok with my daughter, it was ok with me and welcome to the family.

So we now fast forward over a year and the big day has arrived. I am standing at the entrance of the church with the most beautiful girl in the world on my arm doing everything in my power not to cry (didn't work) and all I could think about was that beautiful little girl looking up at me from the crib and saying, "Da Da". It was a whirlwind time for Katie. She had a birthday one week, graduated from college the next and just a few short weeks later walked with me down the aisle and watched me give her hand to the man she loves. I don't believe I ever saw Katie so happy and as I watched them at the ceremony and reception, I knew they were meant to be together. I cried several times that day and night and must admit I have a few tears in my eyes right now.

They are starting a new life together in another state. Katie is getting her Master's degree from Duke University and Kurt is working for a computer company nearby doing some secret stuff for the government. He told me it is all hush hush and couldn't tell anyone any details....not even Katie. I didn't say much, but know if she wants to find out, he will get a taste of those big brown eyes himself and all I can think is God help him.

And that the situation as I survey it...

"Bucket Lists"

I watched a movie recently that really got me thinking. It was entitled "The Bucket List" and starred Morgan Freemen and Jack Nicholson. You would think any movie with those two veteran actors in it would be a blockbuster, but this one touched me in a different way. The storyline was about two guys from totally different backgrounds who end up sharing a hospital room. One is a wealthy businessman with an estranged family and the other a mechanic who raised a number of children and put them all through good schools. While they had totally different lives, they did share one thing, they were both diagnosed with incurable cancer.

Before the diagnoses, they didn't hit it off very well, but after the news came from their respective doctors they seemed to come to a quick understanding of each other's plight. The premise of the movie was unveiled when, in one scene shortly after getting the bad news, Morgan Freeman crumpled up a piece of paper and through it on the floor. It turned out to be his character's bucket list. That is, all the things he wanted to do before he "kicked the bucket". He tossed it on the floor because he felt he could no longer accomplish any of the items he had written down. The paper caught the attention of Jack Nicholson and you can imagine what happened next. The two take off on a worldwide adventure that would keep any viewer's interest. The movie has an excellent storyline, but I couldn't stop thinking about the list. I will hit the magic number 50 next year and while I have done a few things in my life, I have decided it's time to put together my own "Bucket List".

I have been putting a lot of thought into it, but the paper is still blank. I have a few items that came to mind early, but I think Pamela Anderson is already dating someone and winning big in Las Vegas only happens in the movies. Seriously, this list is a concept we should all think about. It doesn't have to contain monumental things, but more importantly, things that truly make a difference in our lives and more importantly, the lives of others.

Some of the items I believe will end up on my list are:

1) Visit the country of Croatia and the village where my grandfather and grandmother grew up.

2) Read bedtime stories to my grandchildren (when I get some) while listening to the waves lap the shoreline of Lake Gogebic (I hope my kids read this).

3) Build a piece of furniture that is truly perfect in every way....and then donate it to charity.

4) Ride my Harley around one or all of the Great Lakes.

5) Make something good out of something bad....like my golf game.

6) Publish a book of all the articles I have written (I didn't say it had to sell).

And so on. I don't believe this is my complete list, but I do think I will transfer it to a piece of paper soon, carry it with me and add to it as something strikes me. I also look forward to being able to check off a few things as completed. This is a good idea for anyone to do. I am sure we all have things we would like to accomplish before we "kick the bucket" and now would be a perfect time to start writing them down and getting them done. I know I will be better for it and you will too. But before I start, I should double check the entertainment news, Pamela could be single again.

And that the situation as I survey it...

"1st Annual Mosinee Grade Event"

As usual, when the leaves start to fall and the temperature starts to drop, my thoughts turn to going to camp. It is somewhat of a ritual for many males across all parts of our country, but none more so than the ones who have Yooper blood in them. Yooper, of course, meaning those of us who were lucky enough to be born and raised in Michigan's Upper Peninsula. It seems that once Labor Day weekend is over, most of the male Yooper population make the usually short trip to camp on Friday night and return sometime on Sunday (usually in time to watch the Packers game). For me, it isn't a short trip. It typically means a 9 plus hour drive, but I somehow don't mind. Just as the geese fly south, I find myself being drawn to the place I grew up and the company of friends of many years.

The weather in the fall is hard to beat. It is still warm during the day, but the nights are cool for sleeping and the bugs have left the area to travel south to bother someone else. The daylight hours are spent on the little odd jobs necessary to keep a camp in order. They may include some exterior repair on the camp itself or on the camp road. They never seem to get totally done because there does need to be work for the next weekend. It is also a time to get the interiors in order as well. Fix a bunk, repaint the floor and tighten the screws on the chairs. They are all important things to do this time of year. Fall is also cleaning time to get ready for the upcoming deer season which is the culmination of all the activities and no work can be done during that time period. At night during the fall it is time to relax and re-tell the stories from times past. The food may not be gourmet, but it is hot and in no short supply. There is usually an adult beverage or two to be had and a card game sometime during the evening. Visiting another camp or receiving visitors at our camp is also a part of the ritual.

The stories told are as good as they were the prior year, but even more special when a new one gets thrown in from some event in the recent past. The truck in the ditch from a late night trip to town that went haywire, the trip to the emergency room to deal with improper use of the hot water in the sauna or the latest political argument can all get added to the master list for years to come. It is one of the special times that puts a big smile on my face and makes it easier to come back to the "real" world and face its challenges.

I was fortunate to be up at camp recently for a new event. It was billed as the "1st Annual Mosinee Grade Bird Hunt and Spaghetti Feed". Two man teams put up a whopping $10 each with the team shooting the most birds claiming the prize (minus the cost of the spaghetti feed, of course). Keep in mind that in my part of the country a "bird" is a ruffled grouse and nothing else. They aren't pats or grouse or ruffed anything....they are simply birds. My brother and I teamed up together and spent the day roaming the trails in my side by side. A side by side is like a quad runner, but on steroids. We had a great time and even managed to shoot some birds. We put about 65 miles on the Rhino, got stuck twice (good thing for the winch) and managed to come in second place out of 12 teams. We didn't win any money but really enjoyed the day. The feed went off without a hitch and there were even a few late night card games. Life was good.

As I was riding around that day, I kept thinking about what my father would say if he were alive. I sure miss him even though he tended to make my life a little rough at times. He wasn't the type of person who liked luxuries, and to him, just about everything was a luxury. I remember him telling me how my grandfather used to hunt with his buddies. They would actually leave their houses and walk to where they were going to hunt. Most of them didn't have a car and if they did, they sure wouldn't waste any hard earned money on fuel to go hunting, especially when you had two perfectly good feet. When I was growing up and hunting with my father, we at least got to drive to where we were going to hunt, but rarely drove more than that. We didn't have a nice 4 wheel drive truck. We had to use the one and only vehicle in the family and it better come home in one piece since Mom had to use it to grocery shop the next day.

All this was passing through my mind as my brother and I were making our way through the woods in my side by side. We were listening to the radio, had a cooler (of soda) within arm's reach and only had to get out to shoot a bird or to answer nature's call. I know if my father were still alive, he would have had a fit over the new toy and how lazy we have become, but my guess is my grandfather wasn't any too pleased with my Dad when he drove us to the woods instead of walking from home. Times have changed, I guess, and I see nothing wrong with embracing new technology especially when it makes your day just a little bit easier. Although, I am sure, in a few years, I will give my son Matt some grief when he pulls up to camp in his hover craft and wants to take me for a ride.

And that the situation as I survey it...

"Let It Snow"

As I sit by my computer today, I have to smile as I look out the window. I am currently in one of my favorite places in the world, my cottage in the west end of Michigan's Upper Peninsula. I am not only smiling because of my current location, but because today is living up to this area's reputation. It is about 10 degrees above zero and the wind and snow are whipping past the window at a rate that prohibits me from seeing even the lake shore about 80 feet away. Some may think I am in need of professional help, but I am smiling because there is a fire in the fireplace, crackling quite happily and the fridge is fully stocked so no matter how intense the storm gets, I have enough supplies to weather it for about as long as necessary.

When I am here on days like today, my mind drifts back to years past. Growing up in this area, I lived through any number of storms, many of them far more intense than the one currently blowing around outside. One of the things all those storms had in common was bestowing on me the ability to weather them by the good graces of my parents and the house where I was raised. My Mom and Dad always made sure their children spent time outside enjoying all the sledding the hills had to offer and along with our friends, we built many snow forts and had all the snowball fights we could handle. But no matter what happened we came home to a warm house, hot chocolate and maybe even some freshly baked cookies. I can still smell them as I sit here today. As the wet coats and snow pants came off, a sniffle would bring a look from my mother making sure it was simply a change in temperature coming from outside to in and nothing more. We would get a fresh tissue and a smile that would warm up even the coldest bones.

If it were a weekend or a holiday, the rest of the day or evening was spent chasing a monopoly piece around the board or watching the same black and white movie on the television we had seen 50 times before. My Mom loves musicals and old movies, so we watched our share growing up. If the next day were a school day, we had to make sure any and all homework was complete before anything else could be done. I can remember sitting at the kitchen table doing homework, watching the snow fall and listening to the wind howl much as I am doing today. Back then, just as today, I had no worries about the storm. I knew Mom had plenty of food in the house and Dad had the furnace in great shape, so we would all be safe and able to laugh at whatever Mother Nature threw our way. I think having it storm outside brought us all closer together in that house on Silver street. If we were really lucky, it would be a bad enough storm that in the morning our local AM radio station (in fact, the only area radio station) would let us know that school was canceled for the day and we could begin our snow adventures all over again.

The hum of the computer brings my mind back to the present and the reason I am working on the computer in the first place, writing this article. I can almost hear my mother's voice telling me to hang up my wet snow clothes in the basement and that the cookies would be ready in a minute. I swear I can smell them as they cool and hear the sound of the water boiling for the hot chocolate. I guess I will be getting up soon to try them out. I am not sure, but I think if I look hard enough I will be able to find a good old black and white movie on the TV today or maybe even one of Mom's favorite musicals. I can't think of a better way to spend a stormy, snowy day in God's country.

And that's the situation as I survey it...

"Bulletproof"

This seems to be one time of the year when I tend to reflect on things that have happened in my life and it seems each and every year the list gets longer. I guess the reason for the reflection is this is my birthday month and even as a young boy I had a number of things to think about. Whether it was my first job or my first kiss from that special girl, the list required a bit of reflection. This year holds an even more significant milestone as it is the year in which I turned fifty years of age and while I don't feel particularly old, it didn't come without some trials and tribulation.

I smile as I think about the wonderful friends I have made over the years and how proud I am of my kids as they are now making their own mark in the world. I get to even add to this part as my daughter married a wonderful young man last year and how special they are together. I hope in future years my list will include some grandchildren and how spoiled their grandpa makes them. I have always been told that's a grandpa's job and I hope I can live up to the challenge. But until then, just reflecting on my kids and their lives makes me extremely happy.

Of course, not everything in my life falls into the positive category and while it causes some pain to reflect on the other column, I would be remiss not to. There are a number of smaller issues that come to mind, but one of relative size is that the kid's Mom and I were not able to stay together. We almost made it 25 years, but building a career and not paying enough attention to those at home certainly contributed to the demise of our relationship. Although we have been apart for about a year and a half, we still communicate pretty regularly (usually about the kids) and we didn't part enemies. The kids' Mom wanted to head in a different direction and I could see it would more than likely make her a lot happier than the direction we were going. We have a lot of good things that came out of our relationship and I like to focus a little more energy on those than any other.

As I mentioned earlier, this was an extra special year because of my big 50th birthday. I have always felt special on my birthday and this year was to be no exception....that is until "it" happened. I was working a charity event a couple of evenings before my big day and when I arrived home, I got out of my truck to open the garage door. After the door opened, I turned to get back to my truck, but to my surprise discovered that the rain earlier in the day had turned to black ice. Much to my dismay I fell forward and rammed my forehead into the side of my truck and was immediately propelled backward and found the concrete driveway with the back of my head. Now totally disoriented, I tried to lift myself up, but was unable to. After a period of time I was able to roll onto the lawn and get myself up and into the house. It was not a good situation as I felt pain from most parts of my body.

The bottom line was the next morning I awoke to being covered in blood and having my left eye swollen completely shut. My lady had come over to my house and was shocked to see me in the shape I was in. I tried to dismiss the whole thing, but at her urging, I found myself in the ER a little bit later and admitted to a hospital in the afternoon. "How could this be?" I thought. "I am bulletproof." Well, long story short, I found out the last thing I am is bulletproof. Two days later I was still in the hospital and although it was my 50th birthday that day, it was obvious I wasn't going to be doing any celebrating in the near future. I did have an opportunity to reflect and can tell you it wasn't my usual list. Having never felt remotely fragile, I was having difficulty facing the reality of my situation. I should be fine over a little bit of time and may even be able to forget most of the bad feelings and only remember how important it is to live life to the fullest as you never know what cards you will be dealt. All I know is I will be far more aware of ice than I ever have been before and that I would like to have many more years to reflect on my birthdays. My hope is that the reflection will be on how much I spoiled my grandkids and not on the wakeup call I got on my 50th birthday. Of course, they will only hear stories about the grandpa's history of being bulletproof and nothing about his inability to handle a simple walk on the ice.

And that's the situation as I survey it............

"Keeping Up"

It makes me smile at times how one thing happening for someone can trigger another thing for someone else. If you think about it, usually it is the "keeping up with the Jones" situation. Essentially, when your neighbor buys a new car (especially a neighbor you may not care for), it moves you to get one as well and usually it is a little bigger or a little fancier. I have a cousin who is famous for that and I laugh every time it happens. One of the first times I was exposed to his way was a number of years ago when my brother bought a small tractor to mow his 25 acres and to perform general tasks around his house. My brother works very hard for what little money he makes at his job, so I know this purchase was difficult for him, but it was a needed piece of equipment. When my cousin found out about Pete's tractor, he had to see it. My cousin has a pretty good job and even though he lived in the city at the time on a standard lot, it wasn't long before he had his own tractor and it was just a little bigger and just a little better equipped. I don't think he used it much until a few years later when he moved out into the country. We all laughed about it and just shook our heads at the sight of the tractor collecting dust in his garage. He never admitted he was a slave to the "Jones", but we knew better. He did finally have to admit his need to have the top stuff when a year or so later he asked me to build a gun rack for his deer camp. I had built several by then for my brother's camp and various friends with deer camps around the area. They were all pleased with the rack's look and functionality. The gun racks were fun to make and time in my shop is a great thing so I had no problem with building one more for his camp. The laughter started though when I asked him what size he wanted it to be and before he could catch himself, he blurted out, "One gun bigger than your brother's." When I finally stopped laughing he did have to admit he was hung up "just a little" with having things bigger, better or more functional than others. I did build him the rack and it is one gun larger than my brother's, but as most good deer camp stories, it gets pointed out every year and we all get to raz him about it and all the other things he has acquired in his life to beat those ole Jones.

The trigger doesn't always have to be a reason to outdo anybody. Sometimes it just makes sense to follow suit or it rekindles a prior thought. This second reason is what I fell victim to recently. My lady Stephanie had talked to me a while ago about getting a small dog and since we spend a significant amount of time together (which I enjoy), she wanted my opinion and buy-in. I lost my best bud, Mickey, a few years ago and thought a new addition would be a great idea, but my current travel schedule could make it difficult. The more we talked about it, the more Steph and I decided to let some time go by and look for the right opportunity. Steph knew the kind of dog she would like and while the little guy wouldn't be much of a hunter at a maximum weight of 10 pounds, I have seen a number of these hybrid pups and their owners always seem to be pretty darn happy. These types of dogs can be expensive (at least more than free, which is what I was used to paying) and the logistics of having her house and my house equipped to accommodate the dog caused us to slowly turn our attention to other things....that is until one fateful day recently when my daughter and son-in-law sent me a picture.

Katie and her husband Kurt live in North Carolina while Katie is getting her Masters at Duke University and Kurt keeps many of Duke's computers humming as an IT specialist there. The picture they sent to my phone had a simple caption. It read "Take a look at your new grandson" and the picture was of a very small, very cute little puppy they were about to get. I have to admit it was a great picture and without really thinking about it, I forwarded it on to Steph so she could see the soon to be new addition to the family. Little did I know the reaction that would result in. It wasn't more than a few minutes after I hit the send button when I got a response from Steph. She wrote how excited she was for Katie and Kurt, but once she saw the picture of the pup, it didn't just rekindle her own desire for a puppy, it was like throwing gasoline on a smoldering fire. I soon became inundated with copies of ads Steph had found online all with the same request...."How about this one?" The puppies in the ads were very nice, but not the kind of pup we had discussed and it became apparent the timing was becoming more important than the original thoughts of type, size and location. After reviewing each ad my response was consistent. I liked the pups in the ads and while I felt they all would be great additions, I more importantly felt we should wait until the right one came to us meeting the details we had discussed and decided on. It wasn't an easy response to send back as I could tell my lady's patience with the process and with me was wearing thin, but I felt it would be worth the wait. As luck would have it, it wasn't long before I got an email from Steph with a picture of a puppy that was exactly the breed we had agreed upon and more importantly the breed which Steph had wanted from the beginning and from a breeder that was very close to us and the price was less than anything we had seen before. I breathed a huge sigh of relief and of course took the opportunity to remind her of waiting for what you want rather than settling was the right thing to do. Ok, maybe I didn't emphasize that very much (I am kind of a chicken at times), but Steph is a sharp lady and picked up on it right away.

So now entering our life is Burley. He was born in February of this year and is a special addition for us both. He is a lot smaller than the hunting dogs I raised over the years, but it is easier to pick him up and have him rest in your lap than a beagle or spaniel. I have to admit that lady of mine is pretty sharp for thinking of getting him, I just hope she doesn't want a tractor sometime in the future.

And that's the situation as I survey it.....

"The Colder the Better"

As I get older, I find myself being at odds with many other people over one thing.....temperature. Most people I speak with really enjoy warmer temperatures. I am the exact opposite. It is "the colder the better" for me. Maybe this has to do with my upbringing and where it was. Most everyone knows the Upper Peninsula of Michigan is about as far from a tropical paradise as one can get, but it does get its share of warm weather every now and again. Growing up, my Dad, who was no fan of hot weather either, would remark that he enjoyed the fact that where we lived didn't really have a summer....only 6 weeks of bad skiing. I also heard him say on occasion that he took his long johns off on the 4th of July, and put them back on July 5th.

We enjoyed our long winters by doing all the things outside we could stand. Sledding, skating, skiing and building snow forts were the items of the day as a youngster. As I got older, I enjoyed snowmobiling, hunting and ice fishing as well. They were all great things to do and rarely did anyone complain about the snow or the cold. In fact, while I was attending Michigan Tech as a sophomore during the winter of 1978-79, we had a record winter for snow. That season 356 inches of snow fell in the Copper Country. That is just less than 30 vertical feet of the white stuff. What I remember the most about it was at one time during that season it snowed 65 days in a row. It was awesome!! I lived on a highway right across from campus and there were days when it was snowing and blowing so hard, you couldn't see the other side of the highway. It made going to class interesting, but classes were never canceled. I think they have cancelled them a few times since then, but the University may be a little more concerned about the safety of their students than they were 30 years ago.

Today it seems that many people just can't take the kind of weather we get. Starting in October the highways are full of people heading to warmer climates for the winter season. I just like to make sure the propane tank is full at the cottage and there is enough firewood cut to keep the fireplace going for as long as I want it to. My lady, Stephanie and I spent the holiday season together at my cottage this year and just had a blast. She is quite the trooper and one of the things that caught my attention when we first met was a conversation about the temperature. She commented she would rather go someplace cold in the winter than someplace warm. That is music to this Yooper's ears. She was true to her word and we had a great time on the edge of the frozen lake known as Gogebic. In fact when we left a few days after New Year's, we were loading my truck with a few things and didn't have jackets on. I did notice it was a little cool, but we weren't spending a lot of time outside and I let it pass. When we got into the truck to head back downstate and turned the key, the thermometer said it was minus 22 degrees. We both felt it was exhilarating and not an issue.

I find areas of hot weather do the exact opposite. The high temperatures drag my energy down and make me extremely tired. I was in South Carolina recently and it was almost a hundred degrees. People were full of smiles as they played on the beach. I was miserable and couldn't wait to find anyplace with an air conditioner. My Dad always said, "You can dress for cold, but you can't dress for hot." How right he was. I thought about those words while I was there and felt the moisture pouring from my system, not sure if I hadn't sprung a leak. I couldn't wait to get back on an airplane and head north. Even though we do get hot temps in the lower peninsula of Michigan, they aren't anywhere near as high as other places across the US.

I guess my future will not be pictured in one of the southern states. I believe I will always find a way to migrate back to my northern homeland no matter what the temperature is. When I am asked why I am not a fan of warm temps, I respond by simply saying, "Fat boys from the UP don't like hot weather and never will."

And that's the situation as I survey it...

"The Joys of Traveling"

I have been doing a fair amount of traveling this year by both plane and by car. I am not a big fan of travel, but it does need to be done. One of the realities of travel makes me smile but also makes me want to throw my carry on through an x-ray machine. This travel reality is infrequent travelers. My frustration is that I don't believe the airlines do enough to educate infrequent travelers as to what to expect when they hit the door of an airport. I have stood in dozens of security lines while people search for their IDs or for their tickets. Even worse is the trip through screening where 2 gallon containers of hair-gel or suntan lotion are attempted to be passed through. Regardless of how many signs are up warning of the rules, I have to stand and wait while this traveler argues with the TSA agent about how harmless the economy sized bottle of mouthwash is and how stupid the rules are. Of course their reasoning falls on deaf ears and after what seems to be an hour, the bottle is tossed in the garbage and the bad breathed traveler gets the line moving once again.

On a recent trip, I was behind a younger lad who had on a backpack while we were in line. When he got to the table just before the x-ray machine he grabbed 5 plastic trays and took his sweet time filling them with just about every piece of techno crap you could imagine. Then to make matters worse he was stopped 4 individual times going through the detector because of a cell phone, spare change, a forgotten belt and a metal business card holder. Even the lady working the machine was getting miffed. She just looked at me with that "I would shoot him if I could" look. I nodded hoping it would give her some type of needed secret approval, but she finally let him through without putting him out of my misery.

This situation isn't a trait of men or women, the young or the not so young or the poor or not so poor. It is simply a situation of people who haven't been on an airplane for a while or ever. In this day and age if you can't demonstrate a history of frequent travel you should have to pass a quiz before you can get your boarding pass. It would be a great place to teach people the rules before they hit airport security. Asking questions about liquids and electronics and baggage could save tons of time and maybe even some dollars in this rocky economy.

Even though these types of travelers can cause some heartburn, they also make me smile. Many of them are traveling for the best of reasons. They may be going on vacation or visiting loved ones or finally getting away for a break. I have watched families who you know saved all year to get away stand in line with ear to ear smiles waiting to get to their destination. I have watched children off to visit grandparents or friends taking that long weekend together to make history of some type. Golf clubs, tennis rackets, fishing poles, video cameras and sometimes just really thick books are the items of choice for making that special trip even more so. I just hope they all pass the quiz and not make me wait any more than I have to while they try to convince the TSA agent to let them carry their blow torch cigar lighter on the airplane.

And that's the situation as I survey it...

"Roasted"

Sometimes it doesn't pay to open your mouth or raise your hand 'cause it can backfire something terrible. This happened to me recently (ok, not the first time) and I am not sure what I am in for. One of my pastimes is community service. I have always believed helping out in your community in any way possible is a good thing. I guess I got this trait from my mother, who at almost 80 still sits on a few civic and church boards. She has been on the school board, the housing commission and the election board just to name a few. Over the years I have and still do as she does. She is a pretty special lady and I usually can't go wrong following her lead… perhaps until now.

One of the boards I have been on for a number of years provides recreational opportunities for adults and youth, especially those that can't afford to participate. The group has been around a long time and every year is able to serve several thousand kids who normally couldn't afford to play baseball or softball or golf just to name a few of the activities offered. There are a number of expenses; so much of what the board does is work with the organization to raise funds to support the programs. It is a lot of effort, but the cause is awesome and it has always been a labor of love for me.

One of the major fundraisers for this group over the years has been a Community Salute dinner for a special person from the area. We have honored many great people over the years and through the generosity of sponsors and attendees have raised significant funds to keep our programs alive. It should come as no surprise that the folks we select to honor usually have a large following that would be conspicuous by their absence if they didn't buy a table of tickets and attend the event. The good news is we have been very successful in both recognizing deserved individuals and raising funds. The bad news is after a number of years we really have to think about possible honorees. It's not that there aren't still many deserving folks who should be honored, it's that in these troubled times, money is certainly tighter and the group of folks with "got-to-be there" followers is getting smaller.

This year was no different. I thought we had come up with a good selection, but an individual who has been a true leader in our area was unable to be a part of the event this year. So we went back to the drawing board. I happened to miss the next meeting due to some travel and when I arrived back in town I inquired about the status of the selection process. I had thought of another possibility, but before I could say anything, the executive director of the organization said the board had met and had come up with a new choice. When I asked who, she said it was me!! I was absolutely caught by surprise. It is a huge honor to be selected for this event, but I really felt for a number of reasons, I wasn't the right person. I asked her if the entire board had hit their collective heads and had they forgotten the purpose was to raise money and the individual selected needed to be easily recognizable by the public for their efforts so we could be sure we would have a good turnout? She assured me the board was perfectly sane and that they actually wanted to change the program slightly and felt I was a perfect choice given the change and would I please say yes. I told her I thought they were still off their rockers and no one would be there but myself and my lady Stephanie (who would kind of feel obligated to go), but given the honor of being asked and the regard I have for the organization and its purpose, I would be foolish not to say yes.

It was then I remembered the part of the conversation about a change, but didn't ask about it until after I agreed to do it. When I did inquire, she said it wasn't a big change, just that instead of a salute; it was going to be more of a roast. "Oh oh", I thought. Now, not only isn't anyone going to be there, but the ones who do come will be there for an evening of humor at my expense. It is still an honor for me to be selected and I wasn't going to back out now, so the planning began.

I really wasn't too worried about the roasting part because I really felt the whole event wouldn't hold much interest for many folks and only a few would show, take their shots and I would be home early licking my wounds, all for a great cause. I can't tell you how wrong I was. Once the word got out about the event and more importantly, the change to a roast, sponsorships have shown up strongly and tickets are selling at a brisk rate. I didn't realize there were so many people lining up wanting to get their shots in on yours truly. I have been in the area for almost thirty years and guess I have done my share of not so bright things, but never thought I would have to re-live them until now. I am told folks are lining up to be on the actual "Roast John's Backside" dais. Now, I am not sure what at all to expect and I can tell you I am just a little nervous....

To make matters worse, the event committee has done a superb job (jeez, thanks) of advertising the event so even the folks who can't go are stopping me in the street just to tell me what they would have said had they been able to be there. I really can't believe some people have such good memories or that my faux pas leave such a lasting impression. I won't forget the whole reason for the evening is to have fun and raise money for a great cause, but now I am just darn worried about what's going to come out that evening.

One good thing is the event committee had made the whole evening a Yooper theme after my beloved homeland, so I will get to eat pasties and drink a little....ok, maybe a lot. I plan to wear my best flannel shirt and have warned a few I may just carry my hunting knife (which is standard Yooper wear) in case anyone gets out of hand with embarrassing stories. I think just the sight of me sharpening the 10" blade on my Bowie knife may be enough to have some of the folks think twice before they recount some of my poorer judgments. By the time you read this, the event will have happened so don't get any ideas about joining in.

All in all, it is an unbelievable honor to even be thought of for this event and although it may be a little painful, the folks that will be there are my friends and sometimes that's what friends do, have fun at your expense. My hope is that we are able to raise some good revenue for the organization's programs and if so, any pain for me will be well worth it. I do plan to have a long talk with my Mom when next I am home and blame her for this. Why couldn't she just play bingo like everybody else? It may cost a little, but not much chance of getting into trouble.

And that's the situation as I survey it...

"Venison can be hard to get"

It is the time of year when the rifles are cleaned and put away and the deer hunting paraphernalia is hung up, locked up or just tossed out as it is the end of this year's whitetail deer season in Michigan. As I have done for too many years to remember, I made two treks back to my homeland in the Upper Peninsula this season with a specific task of bringing home some venison. I have hunted small game since I was 6 and whitetail deer since I was 14 and have been fortunate enough to bag my share of game. As I have gotten older, I am finding more joy in just being in the woods and at deer camp than really worrying about having a successful hunt. That is until this year.

About 6 years ago, I made a conscious decision to pass up any buck that wasn't at least a 6 point and since then have shot a couple of nice 8 points and passed up countless small bucks. I don't mind this at all as it leaves some deer for the young lads that are finding their way to camp these days and I don't have to worry about dragging and cleaning and processing unless it is a nice deer. Instead of being totally engrossed in what is appearing in front of my blind, I can enjoy a good book, text message my office for the latest goings on or as of this year, load my little mini laptop with the phone air card in my backpack and answer email or surf the net some. It is amazing that even in one of the most remote parts of Michigan I can take advantage of such technology. I know, I know, Fred Bear is spinning in his grave and my father is too, but before this season, life at deer camp was pretty darn good. Why not this season? Well that's because this season, there is a new influence on Johnny Big Time....my little lady Stephanie.

Steph and I have been together over a year now and she really brings a lot of joy to my life. We both spend a fair amount of time trying to do nice things for each other and that always puts a smile on my face. One of her favorite meats is venison and at the end of last season when I reported to her I passed on a couple of small bucks, she didn't say it, but I knew she would have rather had the venison, than the hopes of a large rack hanging somewhere. So, I told myself this season I would make her happy and get some venison for the table even if it meant taking one of those smaller bucks I saw pretty regularly. Great plan except for one thing…this year happened to be one of the worst deer seasons in the history of the west end of the UP.

There was little to no deer sign before season and very few buck sightings of any size during this fall's bird season. I knew I was in for some work, but I was up to the challenge. To make matters worse, my fellow camp mates copped an attitude early and decided to have fun in and around camp instead of hunting. In other years I would have gladly joined them, but this year I was on a mission. Opening day, all of us were up early and out the door well before sunrise. Normally, I pack a lunch and hunt dark to dark, but decided to splurge and at least come in for a bite of lunch. From shooting light until 12:30 pm, I didn't see as much as a chick-a-dee and somewhat dejected headed in for some lunch. What I discovered when I got back to camp was my camp mates had quit hunting a few hours earlier and had no intent on going back out to sit and watch leaves blow. They razzed me a bit when I left an hour later to go back to my blind, but I said to myself that I would show them by returning with a buck. Unfortunately, the afternoon hunt was just as fruitful as the one in the morning. I didn't see one single deer until I was about out of light when I saw a doe walk by. Seeing that doe did lift my spirits a little and when I went back to camp I was encouraged tomorrow might be a better day.

I got up early in the morning and although my camp mates were also up, none were planning to hunt...in fact there was talk of a road trip. Usually, I would be the first one to the cooler, but instead I packed my back pack and headed out. The sun came up and the temperature rose until it was just a darn nice day, but still no deer, let alone one with horns. Just before lunch I did see a few does and felt this may be the day. As I headed back to camp, I was caught by surprise. At the camp road entrance, there were three trucks, a picnic table, two benches and my camp mates each holding a beer and a smile. As I got closer I saw a sign taped to a stick at the side of the road. It simply said, "The Mosinee Grade Chamber of Commerce welcomes all Hunters!" When I asked what the deal was, my buds said it was too nice of a day to hunt so they decided to have a picnic instead and I should join them. I thanked them for the invitation, but was going to grab a bowl of soup and head back out. Again, I caught a little grief, but turned a deaf ear to all the fun they were having because I was determined to get a buck. When I came back through the area an hour later, there were 15 trucks there and 25 guys around the fire and someone had run into town and brought back hotdogs and marshmallows. Of course, a few beers had been consumed and the party was really heating up. Despite the invitation to join in, I pressed on. Again, the afternoon brought a few does but no horns of any size to be seen and when I got back I had to listen to the stories of the picnic and the good times had by all. I just grinned and said what a great time I had...watching leaves blow.

And this is how the season went. I hunted hard every day and came up empty while my buds drank, played cards, visited other camps and got visited themselves by others who had decided there were more fruitful things to do than sit in a blind and watch leaves blow. I did enjoy my time in the woods, though. It was fun to get back into the hunt with a serious tone. It reminded me of my early hunting days when it was all about the hunt and nothing else. Even though I came home empty handed this time, it wasn't because I didn't try. Not a bad feeling at all.

My friends did feel sorry for me, but were impressed that I didn't cave in to the peer pressure. My brother even commented I must really like this young lady to pass up all the fun they had. I guess he is partially right. I do think Steph is very special and I feel it will always be that way, but I also rediscovered what it is like to take the hunt seriously and how much fun it can be to plan and think and try to bring home some venison. One of my camp buddies did help me out. His sons had some venison in their freezer and they brought a care package to me for Steph. It was a win-win situation. She has cooked some super venison meals and I have some great memories of my hunt this year. And many of them are more than just watching leaves blow.

And that's the situation as I survey it...

"The Plunge"

I usually try to keep most of these pieces I write on the lighter side. I enjoy when I hear from folks that tell me they smiled after reading my ramblings. Those types of comments are what make it worthwhile to even try to put something together. This edition may be a little different, though. I guess because as of a few weeks ago, I am officially off the market. That's right. I am no longer an eligible bachelor and I am sure hearts across the country are simply shattered.

As I have written a few times, one of my biggest disappointments was having my kids' mom and I split up. That was over 2 ½ years ago and everyone seems to have moved on and no one seems to be terribly worse for the wear. I also have recently written about the lady in my life now and even though it may not seem possible, lightning can strike twice. Stephanie has been with me for almost a year and a half and I can't imagine not spending the rest of eternity with her. So, I thought about it for awhile and decided I wanted to ask her to be my wife.

An easy thing, one would think to ask that question, but I really wanted it to be special and memorable, so I wracked my brain a bit. It came to me around Christmas time. We were spending the holidays surrounded by 4 feet of snow and a crackling fire at my place on the east shore of beautiful Lake Gogebic. Our favorite supperclub the "Root Cellar" has a great New Year's Eve celebration and we made plans to be there. It's a night of good fun, great food, lots of music and celebration. At midnight, after the toasts, there is another type of tradition. Anyone who wants to (and is sober enough to) can climb on top of the bar and on a stool to the timber rafters that support the building. After getting settled up there, you can toast the New Year from a unique vantage spot.

Steph and I had been in the rafters a year earlier and thought it would be great to do it again. What she didn't know was I thought it would be the perfect spot to "pop the question". As it turned out though, just before midnight a friend asked if she could go with us into the rafters as she didn't have anyone in her party with enough liquid courage in them to go up with her. She is a great lady and a good friend so we certainly didn't say no, but it made me re-think my plan as it would have been awkward to have more than just the two of us up there if I was going to carry out my plan. I back-burnered those thoughts and finished the evening with our usual great time.

I spent the next few weeks thinking about an appropriate way to ask for Steph's hand when it came to me. My birthday was just around the corner and Steph was inquiring if I wanted anything in particular as a present for my special day. I didn't have anything in mind at first, but then thought that day could be the right time to put my plan back in place. I told her I did want something special for my birthday. When she asked what it was, I really confused her when I told her I wasn't going to tell her until that day. What I planned was to simply tell her on my birthday all I wanted from her was the word "yes". Since she didn't know what I had in store, she did complain a little that she certainly couldn't shop for something she didn't know about ahead of time, but I assured her it would be made clear on my special day. She just shook her head and made some comment about my sanity. Just another reason she and I fit so well.

That day was approaching quickly and it just so happened we snuck up to the lake (only 550 miles) for the weekend and were again having dinner in our favorite lakeside restaurant. It was just a few days before my 51st and over dinner she asked me once more what my wish was for a present and again I said I would let her know on that day. She gave me the confused look as before, but this time as I looked out the window at the snow falling and the snowmobilers running the lake I realized not only how special she is, but how special this place and the area are to both of us, so I reached over and grabbed her hand and simply said, "Sweetheart, what I would really like for my birthday more than anything is for you to say the word "yes" and make me the happiest guy around." She blinked a couple of times not quite sure what I meant, but in a second or two it registered and much to my relief, she smiled broadly and said "Yes! I would love to be your wife." So there it was. In our most favorite part of the world we became engaged and I know this will set the tone for the rest of our lives.

The date and location of the ceremony have been chosen. It will take place on December 6 of this year and will be held on the deck of "Big Times" which is our place at the west end of Michigan's Upper Peninsula. We already have a judge lined up to do the honors and we plan to have a number of nearby friends and family around us to share in the event. More than likely there will also be just a little party at the "Root" afterward. Steph picked this date and it was also her idea to have it at the place she loves as much as I do. This is just another reason on a long list as to why I love her so much. The date she has chosen would have been her father's 100th birthday. Steph was very close to her dad and although I never met him, I have heard story after story about his zest for life even in his advancing years. He fathered Steph and her siblings later in his life and she credits that with how close they were as he was there for her to share in her life as she was growing up. I can't think of a better day or place to have all this happen.

So if you are in our area over this special day, stop in and join us. You can't miss the "Big Times" sign at the end of our driveway and we would enjoy the company. If for some reason you remember on 12/6/10 what is happening and think about us, simply raise a glass and wish us well. We will hear you. But if you are one of those shattered hearts that I am sure now exists across our great country; please don't put any weird marks or bad words on my picture. I don't look that good in pictures in the first place. I promise to keep it lighter with the next installment and try to make you smile as hard as it might be after getting this news.

And that's the situation as I survey it...

"The Seed King"

I certainly enjoy this time of year. One reason is it brings back so many great memories of the days when I didn't have gray hair and carried school books. This is an exciting time for just about anyone in school. The end of the class year is upon us and whether its graduation from a grade or from a school, it is scary and exciting at the same time. To me, though it always brings back memories of getting that summer job and how difficult it can be and given today's economy, how it hasn't gotten any easier.

As I have written a few times, I grew up in a loving, but certainly not well off household. I learned early if I wanted to try any of the extras life had to offer (like just about anything besides three meals and a bed), I was going to have to earn them myself. I remember my first foray into the entrepreneurial world...I saw an ad in a magazine about selling vegetable seeds. I may have been 8 or 9 at the time and knew everyone in my hometown had a garden and had to get their seeds from someone, so why not me. I envisioned myself becoming the "Seed King" of Bessemer, Michigan and started planning all the places the profits would be spent. My father heard of my plan and had a simple conversation about how tough the competition was and maybe I should look for other ways to make spending money, but the Seed King wasn't having any of it. I had saved enough birthday money to buy the first necessary shipment of seeds (the first of many, I was sure) so off to the bank I went for a money order and then to the post office to begin the wealth enhancement process.

It wasn't long before the seeds hit the front door (in a stylish cardboard sales case, no less) and I was off. I knocked on every door I could find and while everyone was very polite and very understanding about my product, I could tell early on, the Seed King of Bessemer, Michigan was going to be facing an uphill challenge. I decided the best way to face this adversity was to simply knock on more doors and that's exactly what I did. After a week or so, I counted up my fortune and found I had cleared a little more than I had spent out of my birthday money account and decided someone else was going to have to be the Seed King of Bessemer, Michigan because I wasn't having a lot of luck tapping into that market and on top of it all I was missing many hours of great neighborhood baseball, kickball and street hockey games. I didn't make any money playing those games, but I was with my friends and did have a nickel or two in my pocket that I was sure would hold me until the next opportunity for unlimited wealth came along.

I did learn a lot from that experience selling seeds. Even at a young age I recognized the need to be able to relate to the potential buyer whenever I could. It may have been product pricing, quality, timing, past product experience and/or word of mouth, but something either drove the sale or prevented it. Hmmmm, that doesn't seem at all different from the business in today's world. Even though I wasn't able to reach my goal of becoming Bessemer's Seed King, I guess I did take away many valuable lessons not the least of which is I buy my produce from a local grocer so I have a more reasonable excuse if a future Seed King visits my front door.

And that's the situation as I survey it…

"Mr. Guglie"

Do you remember your first haircut? I really don't. I do know for many years my haircuts came from my mom. My parents couldn't really afford to spend the money at a barbershop and Mom was actually pretty good with the barber sheers she bought at a garage sale sometime before I was born. Dad and I both got our trims from my mother until one day when I was about 6 or 7 she said I should get my haircut at the local barber, Dominic "Guglie" Guglielmotto. That truly was his name and this all came back to mind the other day when I was reading my hometown paper online and saw that Mr. Guglielmotto had passed away at age 97. I can't help but remember the day he gave me my first professional haircut.

My mother handed me the 2 or 3 dollars to get my haircut and I jumped on my bike and off I went to his barbershop just a half of a block off the main street in downtown Bessemer. I parked my bike on the side of the building and entered the shop. The radio was going, playing the only radio station available in the area AM 590 WJMS. It was playing at my house too, so it felt as though I hadn't missed a beat. The chair was occupied and someone else was waiting so I simply took a seat and looked around.

The shop was full of displays of combs, nail clippers, aftershave and many other necessary items for the well groomed man. I noticed an award on the wall naming Dominic as a winner of the "Best Flat Top Haircut" in a contest held in Marquette, Michigan in 1957 two years before I was born. I remember being pretty impressed, but I really wasn't interested in a flat top as it was now the mid-1960s and hair was getting longer and less grease was the order of the day. I picked up a recent issue of the magazine "Field and Stream" and began to read about the latest tricks for brook trout success until it was my turn.

When I got to sit in the chair, I was surprised that Mr. Guglielmotto knew my name. I guess small towns do that or perhaps it was the earlier call from my mother to be on the lookout for me. I thought he did a very good job and something felt so good when I saw my reflection in the mirror after he was done. It is hard to describe, but I felt somewhat ready to take on the new challenges of the day with my new haircut. I felt groomed and complete. My mother was pleased when I got home and commented how good I looked which certainly widened my already wide smile.

I went back to Mr. Guglielmotto's shop many times over those next several years and always enjoyed the experience. The shop never seemed to change, but I could always count on reading a good fishing or hunting magazine or overhear some town gossip. Mr. Guglielmotto retired in 1978 after 44 years of barbering, but spent his retirement cutting hair for shut-ins, hospital patients and patients at a medical care facility.

After his retirement he re-discovered his love of downhill skiing and began to ski again at age 66. By the time he gave it up, almost 20 years later for health reasons, he won more than 670 NSATAR downhill ski racing medals with almost 600 being gold. Dominic was featured on 4 TV stations, ESPN Sports and 4 national magazines. That is quite a set of accomplishments for a man from such a humble background and I can't help but be proud that I knew him and had him cut my hair. I have to wonder, though, what that flat top haircut might have looked like at age 6.

And that's the situation as I survey it…

"The Commish"

I have heard a number of times the wise saying "Be careful what you wish for, someday you just might get it" and because of something that has happened recently, I am not sure it isn't true. A few months ago, some friends of mine approached me and asked if I had ever thought of submitting my name for a seat on Michigan's Natural Resources Commission. Before I continue, let me explain a little about the NRC.

Michigan's Natural Resources Commission (NRC) is a 7 member public body whose members are appointed by the Governor. The Commission establishes general resource policies for the Department of Natural Resources and Environment (MDNRE) and by virtue of voter adoption of Proposal G in 1996; the NRC has exclusive authority to regulate the taking of fish and game in Michigan. Now that's a mouthful, I know, but it is an important group to a state that enjoys such tremendous natural resources and game. I was puzzled why I would even be considered for a seat and my friends explained they felt I have a unique perspective having been born and raised in the UP, but having lived below da bridge for the last 29 years. Given that I have hunted, fished and camped all over the state, they felt I could have a positive impact on future decisions of the Commission.

I was certainly honored to be thought of in that fashion, but really felt these guys were standing a little too close to an unlit gas stove. To get a reality check, I had a conversation with my UP buddies over an adult beverage (ok, maybe two) during the opening of walleye season this May at my cottage in the west end of the UP. Keep in mind; most folks in the UP don't have a lot of good things to say about any regulatory group, let alone the MDNRE. So when I mentioned I was being asked to throw my name in for a seat on the NRC, I fully expected to be drug down to the dock and tossed into the lake. Instead, it got a little quiet (which actually scared me more) and finally one of my buddies said he thought it was a great idea. I saw a whole bunch of heads start nodding and smiles come across their faces.

When I asked why they weren't throwing things at me, they pretty much repeated what my friends from downstate had said. "Besides", my Yooper buddies explained, "We know where we can find you when you screw up." Well, who can argue with those words of wisdom? So I spoke to a few folks I know at the state capitol and low and behold, the Governor saw fit to appoint me. This is certainly a tremendous honor, but now that I have been named as the new commissioner, the fun is just beginning.

Even though I have spent my life in the outdoors doing all kinds of hunting and fishing and many other types of recreational pastimes, I am humbled by how little I truly know and I am working hard to learn as much as I can as fast as I can. I receive correspondence and phone calls almost daily on any number of NRC issues from concerned sportsmen and women. I respect the passion and position of all the folks that communicate with me and I spend a lot of time doing as much research as I can to try and understand as much about the topic as I can.

What is amazing to me is how many different groups have been formed across the state to promote their beliefs in a particular part of our outdoor activities. From the Western UP Bear Houndsmen to The Darkhouse Anglers, a prospearfishing group, they are all passionate in their beliefs and simply because I am not a spear fisherman or hunt bear with dogs doesn't at all mean I don't respect their opinions. It simply means I spend the necessary time to understand as much about them as I can.

Actually, it has been a very enlightening and educational experience so far. I have met some great people from all over the state and have learned a lot about a number of different activities, but there is more to learn. I know not everyone is happy with the decisions of the NRC, but I will always try to do the best I can and learn as much as I can. My brother told me recently getting an education won't be a problem as he expects a lot of company at deer camp this year when the locals find out an NRC Commissioner is in town. I think it will be an interesting deer season. Maybe I should wish for early snow and lots of it.

And that's the situation as I survey it...

"The Big Step"

Have you ever planned to do something that was both exciting and a little scary at the same time? If you have, let me ask another question. Did you do it more than once? I suppose you may have thought about that last trip to the amusement park and tackling the latest version of their monster roller coaster or getting on a small airplane on a windy day to travel to an exotic location for a much needed vacation. Those certainly fit the description, but I am talking about something at a larger scale. For those that have children, think back to the day you found out you were going to be a parent and how the smile came across your face at the same time as the butterflies filled your stomach. For many of you, it has happened more than once. Before you jump to conclusions, no I am not going to be a new Dad, well at least not in that fashion. The reason for today's excitement and butterflies is that I am less than a month away from saying the words, "I Do".

The first time I was at this place was almost 30 years ago. It lasted about 25 years and after it was over, I certainly wasn't in any big hurry to do it again. That is, until a couple of years ago when a certain lady came into my life and after a while together, I felt those feelings returning. Feelings I hadn't had in a long time and really wasn't looking to have again. But one thing lead to another and when next I put fingers to keyboard to write the latest edition of these ramblings, I will be an old married man. I am already old, so the other is a simple add-on.

While we are keeping things in perspective as far as a ceremony, there are still decisions to be made and things to be picked out and I find I am taking a more active role than I ever thought I would. My bride-to-be is an extremely intelligent young lady and I love her dearly, but I have spent years learning how to analyze and make decisions without much added delay and I find myself pulling the trigger on things maybe a little quicker than she would like. She is a super analyzer and a deep thinker, and I always tease her that by the time she makes a decision, I had another birthday. It isn't really that bad, but one thing I love about her is we are learning from each other and finding wonderful middle ground on decisions and their timing.

My excitement during this time is all about putting our lives together. We enjoy a vast amount of the same things and experiences. There have been several times where we have gotten lost in our own conversation while in a group setting and have had folks interrupt to get us back into the group conversation. I am very fortunate to have someone like this come into my life.

I guess the butterflies are there because marriage is a big step and I would be more worried if there weren't any. I hope the butterflies are always around along with the excitement that I know will be there. I am not getting on a small plane on a windy day, but I am going to an exotic place with someone I love, for the rest of my life.

And that's the situation as I survey it…

"A One Armed Bandit"

I believe we have all heard stories or had personal experiences of feeling as though someone close that we have lost reached out to touch us in some way. I had just that kind of experience recently. Back in the mid 1960's, my Dad was a Deputy in the local Sheriff's Department. He had that job for several years until he found another one that paid a little better and freed up his weekends. Well, the county jail during this time was built in the 1890s and in everyone's eyes had outlived its usefulness. A new jail was being planned and the old one would be torn down. The Sheriff told my father to get a work crew of some of the "guests" of the jail and start cleaning out the basement of the 80 plus years of accumulation. While Dad was doing this, he spied something mostly buried in one of the corners. As he dug around a little bit, he discovered it was an old slot machine with marking from the early 20s. It wasn't in very good shape and was missing its handle, but I think Dad saw a project in the making.

Dad went to the Sheriff and told him about what he found and wanted to know what he should do with it. The Sheriff didn't know it was there and it more than likely came from some long ago raid and he didn't want it around. It was almost re-election time and he didn't need any of the church goers finding out there was a one armed bandit (minus the arm) residing at the county jail. He told Dad to just get rid of it and that's how it showed up at our house that afternoon. I don't believe Dad was too worried about churchgoers. He spent a fair amount of time working to get the machine back in running order. He had a friend who had worked on old slot machines in years past and they found a handle that wasn't the right one, but it fit and eventually they got it working. I can still remember the old machine in our family room ready to receive any stray nickels from your pocket. As grand kids came along, it became a favorite of theirs to sit with "Grandpa Poncho" and play the slot machine. Dad always had a plastic bowl with nickels for the grandkids, but the rule was all nickels won went back in the bowl for the next visit.

The slot machine hummed along for many years and kids and grandkids alike spent time learning about the finer points to slot gaming. In the late 1980s it stopped working once again and even though he tried several times, Dad just couldn't seem to get it working again. So, it sat in its rightful spot in the family room more as a reminder of a different time than anything else.

I lost my Dad in 1995 and while he wasn't Ward Cleaver, he taught me a lot of things. Besides all things outdoors, he taught me the value of hard work and that of a dollar as well as not being afraid to help friends. I remember sitting around the kitchen table with my family shortly after he passed away and my mother out of the blue looking at me and saying, "Dad wanted you to have the slot machine." Stuff was the last thing on my mind and I really hadn't given the slot machine two thoughts for many years. I was about to offer it to one of my other siblings when my Mom spoke up again and said, "It was one of the few things he spoke of, but he wanted you to have it." That was enough for me and home it came. It has lived in my workshop under a sheet since 1995 until just recently.

Over the years I did some research on it as well as places to repair it, but I just never seemed to follow through, until this year. For some reason, a few months ago, I thought about that machine sitting in my shop all covered up and decided it was time to make it right again. I actually found a restoration expert who was only about an hour away from me and after emailing him for a bit, I knew he was the right man for the job. When I told him I planned to take it back to the Upper Peninsula to be at my place on Lake Gogebic, he thought there was nothing more appropriate than to take it home. I agreed.

About 2 months or so after I dropped it off, I received an email telling me it was complete and ready for pick-up. Along with the email were several pictures of the restored machine and it looked great. Steph and I went down the very next Saturday to pick it up. When I got to Bill's shop and saw his work firsthand, it looked even better than the pictures. He had done a superb job and it worked beautifully. I was thanking him for all his hard work when he asked if I knew about the note. I didn't have a clue what he was talking about. He told me he found a note in the machine and wondered if I knew it was there. I am not sure I was ever inside the machine, so I knew I had never seen a note. Bill smiled as he unlocked the back and pulled out a cigar box full of nickels which were in the machine for some time. In the bottom of the box was a folded up piece of paper that was beautifully handwritten and simply said, "Boys, there are exactly 9 roles of nickels in this box and they are worth $18. There had better be the same amount in this box the next time I check it." It was signed "Dad" and was dated January 30, 1981.

I guess Dad was just protecting his investment. It brought a few tears to my eyes as all the memories of the work he put into the machine over the years and all the work he put into me as well came flooding back. I am not sure why I chose this year to have the slot machine restored or why I didn't go through it myself, but I suspect there was a reason. I also believe Dad still isn't done teaching me a few things and I can't wait for the next lesson.

And that's the situation as I survey it...

"Too Many Gadgets"

I like technology as much as anybody, but it amazes me just how lazy we have become. Forget about the remote control on your favorite 7000 square inch flat screen TV or the programmable thermostat so heaven forbid you don't forget to turn it down at night, or how about the fact that in most restrooms today, you don't even have to flush any of the fixtures. I was traveling to my favorite place in the universe (Lake Gogebic) a while ago and stopped for some gas and a restroom break. As I was leaving the room, something came over me and I stopped. What was odd was I didn't hear the familiar flushing sound. I turned to look at the fixture and lo and behold, it had a handle on it rather than an electronic eye. They actually expected me to turn the handle, I was appalled.

Actually, I was embarrassed that I even expected an auto flush. Leave it to Michigan's Upper Peninsula to bring me back to reality. Some folks would say I was lucky enough to be able to use a flush toilet there and they may just be right. Of course, once I got back into my truck and continued my trip, I became increasingly aware of all the creature comforts I have, even in that truck. It has cruise control which I really appreciate during my 9 hour trip to the lake. It also has OnStar in case I get lost on the same road I have traveled 20 + times a year for the last 30 years. It not only has a radio, but it has an XM radio so I can listen to whatever genre of music I desire or maybe a dose of Blue Collar Comedy. This is totally different than the first trip I made back to my homeland after starting my job in June of 1981. I had to come back home to be in a wedding of a close friend about 6 weeks after I moved to "Troll Land" (aptly named because it is the land where folks live "below da bridge"). What I remember about that trip was there were several stretches of 30 miles or so where NO radio station could be found, either AM or FM. That certainly has changed today even without the advent of satellite radio.

My truck even came with automatic climate control so all I have to do is set the temperature I desire and it heats or cools accordingly. I kind of miss having to play with the fan speed and the temperature lever. I can even have a setting when I parallel park, where the side mirrors tip down to make the view better. I thought that was the ultimate until I recently saw a commercial for a car that will actually parallel park all by itself. Once you pull up to a parking space in the right position, you hit a button and the car does the rest of the work. I watch people try to parallel park all the time and maybe this isn't such a bad idea. I even saw an ad for a car recently that can sense objects and will adjust your speed and/or brake for you.

I guess this thought process better explains the story I read recently about an owner of a new motor home that was in a pretty bad accident. The RV was about destroyed and the owner was banged up as well. After the police got him some medical attention they began to inquire about the cause of the accident. The roads were clear and dry and it was the middle of the day. The RV's owner was just as mystified. He told the police he was taking his new purchase on its maiden voyage and he didn't have a clue as to what happened. He told the officers he had just got on the highway nicely settled in his lane, hit the cruise control button and went back to the galley to make a sandwich. After that, it all went black. My guess is in not too many years we will more than likely be able to make that sandwich without any fear of accident which I guess will be ok as long as I don't lose that remote for the flat screen.

And that's the situation as I survey it...

"Dad's Wall Plaque"

Recently, I had the opportunity to travel through a city I hadn't been to for a long time. I flew into Duluth, MN and rode back toward my hometown with some good friends from California who were going to spend the weekend with Steph and I at our place on Lake Gogebic. Driving through Duluth brought back a ton of great memories from my youth. My Mom and Dad worked hard to support our family, but a school custodian and a part time senior aid didn't have many zeros in their paychecks. We made out fine, but there never was much extra money for things like vacations, so we had to make do.

One way we accomplished that was to look for ways to combine things and a trip to Duluth did just that. One of my cousins had an annual need to go to Duluth to have his braces checked (as orthodontists weren't too plentiful in the UP of Michigan) and Mom and Dad would volunteer to take him to Duluth so he could have his work done. Of course, this turned into our family's one day vacation.

It was only a 2 hour drive to the big city, but you would have thought we were going to cross the desert in a covered wagon. The trip was planned for weeks and a list had to be gone through to make sure we would survive the 120 mile trek to the land of Vikings. The car was thoroughly gone over from an oil change to tire rotation and groceries were set aside to be packed the day we left. Even though we had made this trip for several years, new road maps of Michigan, Wisconsin and Minnesota highways had to be obtained "just in case" some road got moved since the prior year. It took an hour to pack the car making sure all the necessities were included just in case we found ourselves having to homestead some remote area due to car failure.

We would drop my cousin off at his appointment and then head to "Goldfines by the Bridge" which was an early version of Walmart located just into Minnesota after crossing the bridge at Superior, Wisconsin. The aisles were full of things we really couldn't afford, but it was great to travel through the store looking at all the cool stuff. We would then go back and pick up my cousin and head to a department store called "Glass Block" to again look and dream. Occasionally, we would get to pick out a shirt for school, but that was a rare treat.

Off we would go, heading back toward the hometown, satisfied we had seen about the latest everything. On the way back, we always stopped at a cheese shop in Ashland, Wisconsin to pick up some of Wisconsin's finest and take a break from the arduous 2 hour trip we were embarked on. It was one year at this shop, my Dad found something that family and friends still talk about today. Without telling my mother, he bought something and stowed it in the trunk of the car until we arrived home. It was a small plaque to hang on a wall.....a very special plaque.

I need to explain something about my Dad. He wasn't a great people person. In fact, he didn't understand why most people were even around and he didn't do a very good job of hiding his feelings. One of his most disliked times at our house was when we had company, especially my Aunt (my Mom's sister) and her husband who came to town once a year and actually stayed with us for a few days which I know was hell on earth for my Dad. He had strict instructions from my Mom about how to act and even he knew not to cross her, but then he found the plaque.

The wall hanging he discovered in that cheese shop in Ashland, Wisconsin wasn't overly ornate, but contained a message that truly was my father's essence. It simply read, "Relatives and fish stink after three days." I am not sure I ever saw him as happy as when he hung that plaque on one of the walls in our kitchen. Actually, I did see him happier, it was when company would show up and he would find an excuse to get up from his chair and use his sleeve to polish up the plaque as the guests were chatting over coffee. I don't believe it ever stopped anyone from visiting including my Aunt and her husband, but I am sure they all got his message.

That plaque hung in its spot for many years even after Dad passed away and became somewhat of a legend to our local friends and family. I knew one of my younger brothers wanted it, but it stayed in its place until my Mom passed away last year. He went to retrieve it and discovered it was gone. My guess is my Mom at some point thought it was time to retire the plaque and let her guests feel a little more welcome then they were while Dad and his polishing sleeve were around.

I think the tradition of the plaque needs to live on so I went into my woodshop the other day and made a plaque for my brother to have. It is about the same size as the original, but I modified the words slightly. It now reads, "Remember, Poncho always believed relatives and fish stink after three days and he was a pretty bright guy!" I hope it lives on the wall at my brother's for many years to come.

And that's the situation as I survey it...

"A New Family Addition"

Have you ever been warned about something, but did it anyway? Well, that's me and although I don't regret it at all, it has been an interesting decision, to say the least.

My wife Stephanie and I were visiting some friends over a year ago and one of the things Steph wanted to do while we were there was to ride one of our friend's horses. Steph had told me all about her love of horses and how she had a couple over the years, but had sold her last one a while ago and kind of moved on. I told her I understood about having passions, since I probably have too many of them, but horses weren't on my list.

After we had been at our friends' for a bit, Steph and Doreen decided to go riding while Rod and I got caught up on what had been happening since the last time we had gotten together. After a while, we went out to their arena to see how the girls were doing. I have to admit my bride not only had a huge smile on her face, but was doing very well putting the horse through some measures. It was obvious she was in her element and I could see the same passion in her face I see every now and then when I look in a mirror before heading into my woodshop or into the outdoors. When Steph saw me in the arena, she rode over and tried to talk me into getting on a horse. I had to quickly remind her that the last time I was in a saddle the horse was tied to an aluminum pole and went around in circles...slowly. I appreciated the invitation, but told her this horse ride was her thing and I was more than happy to be a spectator. She heard me, but wasn't really listening as she took off for another round with the horse.

On the way home that evening, Steph was still wide eyed and fully into the ride she had that day. She had warned me of her passion for horses and although she didn't even hint at it, I knew what I had to do. I looked at her and said it wasn't fair for me to so many things I love to do and she at least not have one. She kind of blinked and asked me what that meant. I told her if she could find a horse reasonably priced and a place to board it that didn't put us in the poorhouse; she ought to look for a horse of her own. I guess I didn't have to say it twice!!

Within the month, Steph had found a great deal on both a horse and a boarding stable and it was well within our budget, in fact a lot less that I had imagined. So, she now heads off to the barn many times during the week, to see Kingston (the other man in her life) and I have a whole lot more mail to carry in from the various places horse people belong to or buy from.

I have to admit I have also learned several things about the Equine world, whether I wanted to or not. Kingston is a "Foundation" Quarter Horse and I guess that's good, if you like Quarter Horses. I know the vet has to come to see him for various reasons as well as a blacksmith. He has more blankets than I do and Steph has been saving so he can go into training during the coming months to become a better horse, whatever that means. I still have a clean house, hot meals when needed and the love of a great woman, so it is pretty hard for me to complain, other than the occasional tease. It is especially hard for me to complain when I am heading north to go hunting or to my shop to make some saw dust or to the course to play some golf. Fair is fair and so far, it has worked out very well. She still has that beam on her face when she is heading to the barn and after she gets back which warms my heart every time I see it.

The only time I get nervous is when she discovers some new potential for her pride and joy such as mounted shooting competition. She is already a great shot and I don't ever want to make her mad when she is armed, so I am looking for a better potential competition more in tune with my comfort zone, such as Kingston being secured to an aluminum pole and going around in a circle....slowly.

And that's the situation as I survey it...

"The Graduate"

It looks like another milestone has become part of my life. It is certainly not a bad one at all. In fact, it is one that makes me smile and feel good inside. By the time you have a chance to read this; my son, Matthew will have gotten his college degree. It is an Associate's degree, but he is anxious to add a couple more years to it and have a Bachelors' degree to go along with this one. Either way, I am a pretty proud Dad right now. Matthew took a little longer to figure out which direction he wanted to go, but I have to give him credit, when he did figure it out, away he went.

Matthew has been employed for a while and will continue to work for Whirlpool after graduation in their R & D area. What does that mean? I am not sure, but I can tell you when he was in the Dishwasher Division, whenever he came home, he never failed to point out that my dishwasher was originally on one of Columbus's ships and should be replaced. Considering it still did a fine job of cleaning what I put in it and I never pushed any other button than "Normal Wash", I didn't see a need to upgrade. In fact, I encouraged Mr. R & D to use his class skills and simply bring mine into the 21st Century. For some reason, that never seemed to happen.

He now works in the R & D side of washing machines and of course, the one at my house isn't up to par either, but my clothes are clean and it doesn't owe me anything, so I think I will wait to get the new space age version of laundry care after hitting the Mega-Millions.

Matt did a great job of taking some classes that have really helped him at Whirlpool. He has developed a mechanical side as he has taken a number of real shop type classes working with metals. He told me one of the attributes his bosses like is that he can not only design a part using CAD, he can also use a metal lathe to build the darn thing. I think that's great and it sure gives him a set of assets that could be valuable to him throughout his career.

Our conversations lately have also been on a different level. Instead of listening to him tell me about the latest video game, we talk about corporate issues and the economy. He has always been a wide thinker and his views many times are pretty interesting. Of course, we still have to include some latest You-Tube video that he has put together. I am not sure what You-Tube is, but it sounds pretty cool.

Matt also isn't afraid to take on some unusual tasks. He told me recently he volunteered to take part in a program to reverse mentor some of the company execs. Whirlpool thought it would be a good idea if some of their white collar types with gray hair learned a little more about what the younger generation is all about, so Matt was charged with teaching one of the company VPs all about social media. He told me it was fun to take the VP down the learning path of FaceBook, Twitter, You-Tube and a couple others I have never heard of. He said he made a new friend in the VP and they had a good time exchanging ideas. Maybe I should ask him for the same lesson as I am sure all my "peeps" are on the edge of their seats wondering what I had for dinner last night.

I am not sure where life's journey is going to take my son, but if you allow me to boast a little, I have never seen him more ready for the trip. I have always been proud of my children and seeing this new chapter begin, makes me smile that much more. Now if I could only get him to explain that Twitter thing to me.

And that's the situation as I survey it...

"Facebook"

I can't believe I am going to admit this, but I did something recently that I had never done before. No, it didn't involve a unicycle or a roman candle. I think I have already done those. Nope, I recently posted my very first "status" on Facebook. I couldn't help it. I had to defend my weekend. I know that sounds crazy, but let me explain.

Steph went to the UP recently with one of her girlfriends to ride horses at our friends' ranch north of Ironwood. I knew I would be a third wheel, so I decided to stay home for the weekend and get some things done in my shop. I am pretty busy creating things lately for folks who actually want to pay for them and just took in a new commission for a walnut hope chest that needs to be done in short order, so it was the right thing to do.

I have mentioned before that I don't know diddley about social media and really haven't had the urge to learn. Well, Steph talked me into having her post pictures of some of my projects on "our" Facebook page as she thought it might spur some interest. Actually, it has and I have gotten several commissions from those pictures. So of course, I had to activate Facebook on my phone in case someone asked about a project and I wouldn't have to bother Steph to go back and forth with questions and answers.

It really wasn't a big deal until I also started getting all kinds of "status" updates from people on "our" page that I really didn't understand. My bride was also updating her "status" regularly which led me to what I am talking about. It seems that the day she left the lake to head back downstate, she put on her status that she was heading home to see what kind of trouble I had gotten into while bach-ing it over the weekend. That post set off a string of others chiming in on what it was that I could have done. I let it go for a bit, but couldn't hold back any longer. I put on my own inaugural post that said I had spent the weekend in the shop getting work done like any responsible individual and there weren't any shenanigans taking place. Well, that ended the questions and I guess I felt vindicated.

While I was in the shop all weekend and did get a ton of stuff done, I don't sleep in there and I do need nourishment, so I did roam out a little and had a few adult beverages in the evenings. No one on Facebook had to know that. It was only my business...although I did send a text to Steph after I got home one evening asking her where the floor polish was since the dancing girls were on their way over, but for some reason I didn't get a response. Now that I think about it, maybe that's how her status post about me got there in the first place.

It's a good thing I don't know how to do much on that site or I could have some Facebook issues the next time I am left at home to work in the shop.

And that's the situation as I survey it...

Made in the USA
San Bernardino, CA
10 December 2015